Secrets From Behind the Wall

Collected Letters from Prisoners the World Over

By
Don Clair

www.SecretsFromBehindTheWall.com

SECRETS
FROM BEHIND THE WALL
Collected Letters From Prisoners The World Over

Copyright© 2007 by DON CLAIR

This edition was produced for on-demand distribution
by Published By You Distribution Service
ISBN: 978-0-6151-3992-0
FIRST EDITION 2007

For information address:
Don Clair
www.secretsfrombehindthewall.com
Post Office Box 264
Waterloo, IL 62298

Dedication

This book is dedicated to:

Anthony (Tony) Robbins, whose inspiration and belief in me created an exciting movement. He took the time to see what others could not, in men and women who were incarcerated. One of Tony's gifts is that he doesn't see people as who they are, but by who they can become. My dream was to create a residential program in prisons. He put his arm around me and said, "Don, I know you will make it happen." It became real 30 days later.

My devoted wife, Jane, who allows me cave time!

My sons, Thomas, Michael, Matthew and beautiful daughter, JoAnn... each guards a part of me.

Table of Contents

Acknowledgements

I wish to acknowledge Dr. Patti Coffee, Director of the Anthony Robbins Foundation. Her tireless efforts have touched so many lives and often is the glue that holds projects together.

Marcella Vonn Harting and Cay Villars for being at Oak Hill Correctional Center; believing change is possible for anyone and helping me create possibilities for these men and women behind walls.

Mary Campbell and the Rosebud Foundation; they continue to provide services to those that want to make this a better world.

Ann McIndoo, my writing coach and friend, who got my ideas out of my head and onto paper and helped me make this book come alive.

Dee Coppola and Wet Apple Media whose wisdom and insight I cherish. Thanks.

And especially, to all the inmates that have learned the reasons behind their mistakes. God bless them as they reach out to prevent a lesson learned by one of them from happening to someone else.

Foreword

In life there is nothing more powerful than finding the answers to our questions about life itself. When you want to know how to do something new, the answer is a lot easier than our search often seems. If you'll just learn to model the behavior of people who are successfully doing what you want to do, your predictable results will be successful too. Fortunately, this pattern of behavior (modeling) is the quickest and most accurate way to get successful results.

Even when you want to learn how to avoid certain experiences and painful events, all you have to do is take a close look at someone that got the results you want to avoid and model the direct opposite. Notice their behavior and strategies for being where they are and simply AVOID that behavior and those choices.

Because modeling will always create a specific result, it often can serve as the greatest warning. As we look at the number of young adults facing time in our criminal justice system we cannot help but ask, is there another possibility? Are there other alternatives? Does our encouragement of modeling mislead our youth? I mean, after all, they are modeling someone or something.

Once every 50-75 years a startling revelation of how we could have done it better comes along. The difference it makes is immeasurable. Well, that revelation is here and it is a must read for every parent, youth worker, and youth alike.

In Don Clair's, SECRETS FROM BEHIND THE WALL, he brings us a fresh perspective on how we are doing. From his extensive experiences within the prison systems across the United States and abroad, he has learned a powerful method for introducing the work of modeling to our young people. Until now, no one has effectively offered to use the voices of those behind the wall, (who have modeled unsuccessful behaviors) as a launching pad for teaching our youth what to consider when they model behavior.

The truth is that modeling works for everyone. And everyone does it at some level. Our youth, who are most impressionable, however, are not even aware that in almost every instance they are modeling the behaviors of others – That is until now!

With Don's latest work, our youth can read the strategies, thought patterns and described behaviors of people who have made unsuccessful modeling choices. Through these voices— described in collected letters from prisoners the world over, they will hear a plea to focus, to choose wisely, and to consider from moment to moment what they are modeling. From the experts of: "having done it incorrectly" comes great strategies for avoiding the pending doom of life without parole, death row and lost years behind the bars of dreadful modeling.

Dr. Christopher Eaddy Ph.D.

Introduction

The Purpose of the Book

Put yourself in front of the television any night of the week and you see a young person shackled, being put into a police car. You ask yourself these simple questions: "What went wrong with this kid? What went wrong this time? Where are their parents?"

When do you take a stand? When does life present circumstances that one says, "Enough, we have to do something! Someone must reach out. If I don't reach out, who will?" To state the reason behind this book, the matter simply became a "MUST" for me.

I spent most of my adult life working with inmates behind walls of stone and razor wire. I retired in 2000. I wanted to walk away from that kind of life. And I did, for a few days. But, something inside me said that I couldn't retire. I see kids waiting to go to prison. I see adults not doing what they need to do as parents. Not because they don't want to but because the parents truly have no idea what is driving or motivating their child's behavior.

Currently, there are 2.3 million inmates incarcerated, both men and women. Think of it, 2.3 million men and women in prison! Statistically, most of them have 2 to 3 children. That puts nearly 10 million children in the foster care system or with other family members because their parents are incarcerated.

Children of these incarcerated individuals have life tough enough with being labeled dysfunctional due to parental heritage. It's sad but true that these children, and many others like them, are often simply discarded as if they had no more value than an oily rag. As you may know, a fireman's greatest fear is a fire started by spontaneous combustion from oily rags in a pile. Once the fire begins, the flames envelope everything in their path. That's how close we are with anarchy in this country and we don't even know it. Think of it, 10 million oily rags piled up just waiting to internally combust into flames and engulf everything in their path!

I chose to begin a new process to help educate parents and young adults about what they need to live a life outside of the prison walls and razor wire. I chose to do this by using my observations of incarcerated men and women over the last thirty years and pass their lessons on to someone who may face the same choices.

It has been an amazing journey, one that I would never have believed possible for me if it hadn't been for one person. A rather special mentor crossed my path and he chose to allow me to learn from him. His name is Anthony Robbins. I first met Tony because I set a goal to have Tony speak to a group of inmates that completed his Personal Power Program. Tony took me under his wing and provided opportunities to learn and stretch myself.

Tony provides us with a tool to understand what really drives human behavior. He calls it the Six Human Needs. Once I fully grasped the power of the Six Human Needs and how it created a map for why we do what we do in life, I used it to reach those that in the past had been unreachable. Each of us makes choices. These choices rule our lives. They can create markers for future results, either powerfully magical moments or powerfully painful stabs.

The following pages contain warnings from individuals inside the walls; those that have found ways to heal, and simply want to reach out to others. Their deepest wish is to make what they've learned reach the outside world. They want to touch a hurting child, maybe one of the 10 million on that oily heap. I have read thousands of letters from inmates telling me the one thing they would need to have heard to keep them out of prison. From those thousands of letters, the "one" thing they were desperately searching for falls into one of six categories that we call the Six Human Needs.

As I read the letters and discovered their connection to the Six Human Needs, I shared this with Tony, who inspired and guided me to write this book. The letters enclosed will touch you in a unique way; some will make you cry, some will scare you, some will enrich you, all of them will share a secret. Share this secret, this lesson learned the hard way, with your children and other parents.

The Six Human Needs can be simply defined as six instinctive needs—six psychological wants that affect all human behavior. These wants are deeply seated in each human being and as human beings we subconsciously and instinctively seek to experience these needs. These needs are divided into two parts. The first four of our needs can best be described as the Needs of our Personality. The need to experience:

Certainty/Comfort

Variety

Significance

Love/Connection

It has been my observation that individuals that have met these four basic needs fully, are not happy. Something inside always drives them to an internal question that asks, "Is there more to life?" The answer is yes. The two additional Needs that must be met in order to feel life's richness fully are in the area of Needs of the Spirit. The Need to experience:

Growth

Contribution

All human behavior is Needs driven. My daily behaviors are driven by these six human needs. Behavior becomes the means or the Vehicle to experiencing the Human Need. If one goes to the store, the outcome might be to get a loaf of bread. The store holds the bread. We have an internal store where our needs and feelings are kept. Getting to the store (vehicle used to get there) is an individual choice. A skateboard, a bicycle, or an expensive car can be used as the vehicle to get to the store. Any of the vehicles will get me to the store to purchase my bread. It simply becomes a matter of how I choose to get to the store. Will my vehicle get me there fast, slow, in style, with pain or without pain? What vehicle will I choose to use, as the means to experience that need intuitively?

When we examine the notes and letters written as, "Secrets from behind the walls," look at the vehicles the inmates used to meet their Needs. Ask yourself, did they use a broken skateboard or did they use a Cadillac to find that instinctive need? What is the behavior used to meet the Need? Examine the behavior and you will know the need.

Parents, read this book with your kids. Students, when you read these letters, put yourself in the writer's shoes, if only for a moment. Step into what they are trying to tell you – see where it could take you in five or ten years.

Pass these secrets on. That is their wish.

Don Clair

Forgiven

Sitting here feeling lonely and bored
Thoughts of home in my head are stored
Dreams of days when I was free
And realizing all that's ahead of me

I'm scared of the road that's ahead
With death constantly over my head
I want to go back to my ordinary life
Living each day without chaos and strife

I took my freedom for granted
Always asking for more than what was handed
I no longer spend time questioning why,
I'll never know so why bother to try

My life is too short to waste on resentment
So I strive for peace and contentment
As I sit and ponder lost hopes and dreams
I just thank God I'm alive after all I've seen

I need to remember all I've been through
'Cause from this experience I've learned and grew
The time I've spent under D.O.C. (Department of Corrections) rules
Has taught me things I could not learn in school

I did not cause all the anguish or pain
So I can't continue to live my whole life in shame
What occurred was tragic, there is no doubt
Forgiven I am, inside and out

Kelly, Death Row
Metro State Prison, Atlanta, Georgia

CHAPTER ONE
Certainty

"The quality of your life is always defined by the amount of uncertainty you can tolerate."

—Anthony Robbins

Secrets about Control

Some very negative ways to achieve control that both inmates and teens use are telling lies, intimidation, making unrealistic demands, demanding respect, belonging to a peer group that has no expectations (some might call this peer group gangsters), using drugs, and selling drugs. Drug use gives the feeling of control and power. Often this leads to the thought pattern that the one with the most drugs has the most control and power. The above vehicles (behaviors) used to gain the feelings of control are all examples of a "skateboard" or "bicycle" way to achieve that control which gives certainty. Yes, you may feel like you're in control for the moment. However, the class or type of vehicle (behavior) used to get the control is really the secret to experiencing certainty to the fullest. Here are some examples of vehicles (behaviors) used to achieve control and give certainty that have higher standards:

- Doing the right thing
- Getting a good education
- Being flexible
- Being exactly where I tell my parents I am going to be
- Doing exactly what I say I will do

That's called reliability - understanding that boundaries are defined as the laws of society. **These boundaries create control, giving society security.**

One of the most profound things about the need for control that provides comfort is the wisdom to understand that there really is no control. Do you remember where you were on 9/11? In one heartbeat, all the control we thought we had, disappeared. The wisdom in this, as Tony says it: "The quality of your life is always defined by the amount of uncertainty you can tolerate." Our ability to live within that uncertainty creates certainty and new possibilities. To reach beyond what most of us would even dare, in our "bicycle" mode.

Defining certainty is less difficult when we begin to watch behavior. By observing what a person does, we can determine what need they are tying to fulfill. Therefore, certainty is more definable by observing behavior. Behavior is the vehicle used to fulfill the need.

If I had to give you one example, this is what I would tell you to use. Look inside your heart and find what you believe the word trust means. Create a life of trust. Surround yourself with individuals that are trustworthy. When you understand that control means trusting that you have made the right choice, you have endless possibilities. You will live your life this way. You will do everything you can to make your boss look great. By doing that, you will create endless possibilities. When you do everything in your life to create trust and loving relationships for the people closest to you, you have unending possibilities and an abundance of boundless love.

What Is Certainty?

Certainty is the belief that you are in control of a situation. It is that emotional place that you feel that you have control. I'm safe; I'm secure. Sometimes, you'll see that with a teacher who might micromanage you, who really comes down hard on you, because they're trying to create control for a whole classroom. In the real world, bosses micromanage you.

In life, parents do their best to protect their children as they grow into adulthood. Boundaries are a tool or method parents use to meet the need of control to feel like they are doing a good job of creating security/certainty for their children. When parents set boundaries to meet the need of control in teen relationships, it is almost always with the intention of keeping the teen safe. On the other hand, the teen experiences this as being held back in life. They believe that they are grown up enough and will be ok without all the boundaries. It's the dance of life between the fine line of being free to experience life and being controlled to be secure and safe. Learning how to find your way along this line is often like a minefield full of bombs set by parents and teens yelling, "DON'T DO THIS."

The answer to this problem is to learn to become trustworthy. The behavior you give should be worthy of someone trusting you.

As a father, I wanted to trust all of my children. Yet, I knew that each was experiencing special challenges to explore their boundaries. Sometimes these tests come disguised as peer pressure to use drugs or alcohol. One of the most valuable lessons I learned, as a parent, was to make it a point to always give them a hug whenever they came home from an activity. No matter what time they came home. They knew they would have to give me, their father, a hug before they could go to bed. Years later, my sons told me that "goodnight hug" was their way out for many things they did not want to do but their buddies wanted them to do.

Letter from Rochelle

To whom it concerns,   08-29-06

        Hopefully all of you who are listening can hear and relate to what I am motivated to say. My name is Rochelle.   I am a woman, mother, sister, friend and lastly a state prisoner. Life wasn't suppose to end up this way, all I wanted to do was have fun, pay my bills and find someone to love. My wants aren't what led me behind prison walls my reckless choices did. As I sit here thinking of advice for you that may help guide you in a better direction than where I now live with no freedom I stumble for the right things to say. Since no one is perfect and my words come from lessons learned the hard way I will say this: As humans we are going to make mistakes; some big others small however each one of them come with a message to bring. The message can serve for your betterment or your downfall, It's up to you. I challenge you to sit down and look at the mistakes of the past and use them to your advantage. ~~[scribbled out line]~~ Turn a negative experience into a positive picture. Start small and work towards a better you. Next, believe in something bigger than yourself, whether it is God or your inner trust. I hope you learn to trust and believe in yourself. I didn't, instead I listened to peer pressure, expectations and self doubt. Find courage to stand amongst the fallen. Trouble in the past doesn't mean your life is over. You are young, now is the time to live a stronger life. What's stopping you, but you?

With Love and Care,

Rochelle

L.A.S.P (A.B.B)
P.O. Box 709
Alto, Ga 30510

write if you'd like

To Whom It May Concern,

Hopefully, all of you who are listening can hear and relate to what I am motivated to say. My name is Rochelle. I am a woman, mother, sister, friend and currently a state prisoner. Life wasn't supposed to end up this way, all I wanted to do was have fun, pay my bills and find someone to love. My wants aren't what led me behind prison walls, my reckless choices did. As I sit here thinking of advice for you that may help guide you in a better direction than where I now live with no freedom, I stumble for the right things to say. Since no one is perfect and my walls come from lessons learned the hard way, I will say this: As humans, we are going to make mistakes, some big others small; however, each one of them come with a message to bring the message to your mind for your betterment or downfall. It's up to you. I challenge you to sit down and look at the mistakes of the past and use them to your advantage. Turn a negative experience into a positive picture. Start small and work towards a better you. Take control and be responsible. Next, believe in something bigger than yourself, whether it is God or your inner trust. I hope you learn to trust and believe in yourself. I didn't, instead I listened to peer pressure, expectations and self-doubt. Find courage to stand amongst the fallen— trouble in the past doesn't mean your life is over. You are young, now is the time to build a stronger life.

What is stopping you?
With Love and Care,
Rochelle

What is Rochelle's secret and message to you?

If you read Rochelle's message closely, you will notice that she asks you to stand with courage "amongst the fallen." Perhaps she advises you to look at your peer group because it is often a reflection of how you see yourself. The vehicle of learning from your mistakes to manage your emotional state is a true test of power. And when you blend this with a strong belief in spirituality and faith you have opened new possibilities for yourself.

What did you take from this message? What will you do in your future to create Certainty in a positive way?

_____

_____

_____

Letter from Danny

To whom this may concern:

I don't know if there is any one thing that somebody could of done to help me avoid these circumstances. There are times in our life that we feel invincible and that everything we do is the correct way or the only way. And most definetly, if you are reading this, your understanding of what was correct isn't always true. People can't give you anything that you need unless you truly want it. If I could give any one thing to someone that could help them start to understand the circumstances in their life; it would be this one word. Accountability. Be accountable for all of your actions and understand that these actions all have consequences. The biggest lesson that I've learned in this life is that it doesn't matter what you have in life, its who you have in it. Family doesn't have to be blood relatives. The ones who you expect to kick you while your down will be the ones to help you back up. Listen and never say never. When you tell yourself that you can't, you might as well not even try. Accountablity. Education is oppurtunity. Oppurtunity is your chance.

Respectfully

Danny

To Whom This May Concern:

I don't know if there is any one thing that somebody could of done to help me avoid these circumstances. There are times in our life that we feel invincible and that everything we do is the correct way or the only way. And most definitely, if you are reading this, your understanding of what was correct isn't always true. People can't give you anything that you need unless you truly want it. If you could give any one thing to someone that could help them start to understand the circumstances in their life, it would be this one word. Accountability. Be accountable for all of your actions and understand that these actions all have consequences. The biggest lesson that I've learned in this life is that it doesn't matter what you have in life, it's whom you have in it. Family doesn't have to be blood relatives. The ones who you expect to kick you while your down will be the ones to help you back up. Listen and never say never. When you tell yourself that you can't, you might as well not even try. Accountability. Education is opportunity. Opportunity is your chance.

Respectfully,
Danny

What is Danny's secret and message to you?

Wisdom can come from the most unusual places; and sometimes if you really want to learn the secrets of life, simply listen to someone that has lost most of their life. Danny does his best to advise that when we hold ourselves accountable, it provides a sense of control over life. Danny warns about living our lives without understanding we are accountable. This letter comes to you from the depths of darkness inside a place reserved for those doing a life sentence or more. His vision is for you to grasp hold of only one word in life, ACCOUNTABILITY. This one word will provide you a sense of controlling your own life, thus, your destiny.

What did you take from this message? What will you do in your future to create Certainty in a positive way?

_____

_____

Letter from Q

6

What's happening lil Homie, I'm "Q" in Hancock State Pen And Been in At the Age of 15. The things you Doing, I miss those things ; wish I Could Turn Back the Hands of time, But It Can't Be Done. So tighten your lil Ass up ; Fly Right, Because this place will Turn you Into A MAN ; you will Go threw things that No MAN Should Go threw. I'm 24 Years old (You Do the Math), Listen to your Parents ; Away From Peer Pressure, Please! I'll Holla, On Out.....

"Q"

This is "Q,"

What's happening lil Homie, I'm "Q" in Hancock State Pen and been in since the age of 15. The things you doing. I miss those things & wish I could turn back the hands of time. But it can't be done.

So tighten your lil-ass up & Fly right because this place will turn you into a MAN & you will go threw things that no man should GO threw. I'm 24 years old (you do the math), listen to your Parents & away from PEER Pressure, Please!!! You be the MAN.

I'll Holla, Om out...
"Q"

What is Q's secret and message to you?

The lesson "Q " is sending is that society can be unforgiving, even to a 15-year-old. The lessons he fears you will learn are fears only the dark side can create. His message is that controlling your peer group will create your destiny. Please choose wisely!

What did you take from this message? What will you do in your future to create Certainty in a positive way?

_____

_____

_____

Letter from Stephen

Direct message from behind the wall.
Stephen

I felt the best message is to let you
know life behind the wall is. The fact of
having someone telling you your every move
sucks. When to go to bed when to go to
mainline. I wouldn't allow my dog to
come here the pits. I rather be home
than here this is no place for anyone
at all. I miss freedom! The freedom to
do as you please, but not here. Being away
from your love one's. Not know whats going
on out there in the real world. So I
tell you this stay out of prison. Believe
in God and trust no one.

I felt the best message is to let you know how life Behind the Wall is. The fact of having someone telling you your every move SUCKS. When to go to BED, when to go to mainline, turn on the lights, turn off the lights, when to shower and on and on. I would not allow my dog to come here into this pit. I rather be home than here. This is no place for anyone at all. I miss freedom. The freedom to do, as you please, but not here. Being away from your loved ones. Not knowing what is going on out there in the real world. So I tell you this, STAY OUT OF PRISON. Believe in God, and trust no one.

Stephen

What is Stephen's secret and message to you?

Stephen's message is that giving up total control to someone or something results in massive pain. Having no control for many is the ultimate punishment. He offers you one thought that may help on your journey, "believe in God and yourself."

What did you take from this message? What will you do in your future to create Certainty in a positive way?

29

Letter from Alicia

8/29/06.

My name is Alicia. I'll be 47 in Dec, 2006. I've been incarcerated since I was 35. I am serving 35 do 17 years in prison for 2 cts. of First Degree Veh. Homicide. I had cocaine in my system. An off duty policeman died. For him I got 15 years. For his wife 2 years.

I started smoking pot when I was eleven. I graduated to herion & cocaine. I was a drug addict for 26 years.

But the thing, I think, that made me ~~wh~~ want to be a drug addict was because I didn't have an ~~identy~~ identity. I was a non-person. A kid who just happened to live with a mom & dad sister & brother. I never told anyone how alone I felt when I was little. I was embarrassed that I was lonely & had questions.

I say this now: Question everything! If you don't understand ~~something~~ keep asking. Talk to your family, ~~talk to~~ school counselors — Talk to spiritual advisors. Know — that you are an important member of the human race & that you matter much!

Especially, know this:
"God knows the plans He has for you
Plans to give you & good future & a hope."
Jer. 29:11
An He knew this about you before you were born.

♡ Alicia
L.A.S.P

My name is Alicia I'll be 47 in Dec. 2006. I've been incarcerated since I was 35. I am serving 17 years in prison for 2 acts of First Degree Vehicular Homicide. I had cocaine in my system. An off duty policeman died. For him I got 15 years. For his wife, 2 years. I started smoking pot when I was eleven. I graduated to heroin and cocaine. I was a drug addict for 26 years. But the thing, I think that made me want to be a drug addict was because I didn't have an identity. I was a non-person. A kid who just happened to live with mom and dad sister and brother. I never told anyone how alone I felt when I was little. I was embarrassed that I was lonely and had questions. I say this now: Question everything! If you don't understand something, keep asking. Talk to your family, talk to school counselors - talk to spiritual advisors. Know that you are an important member of the human race and that you matter much! Especially know this: God knows the plans he has for you. Plans to give you a good future and a hope. And he knew this about you before you were born.

Alicia,

Georgia State Prison

What is Alicia's secret and message to you?

Alicia offers a powerful lesson about certainty. When you are uncertain about anything, one of the best ways to create certainty is to simply ask questions. Finding the answers provides you with positive ways to deal with those uncertain feelings in life. Alicia chose to find her answers in drugs and for a while they did provide her with answers, but they were not solutions. The answers provided only created addiction. Her most powerful statement was about experiencing life as a non-person. Having no identity will place you on a constant path to find who you are. So she asks, "who are you now?" Her response, "I am an important member of the human race that matters much."

What did you take from this message? What will you do in your future to create Certainty in a positive way?

_____

_____

Closing Thoughts

A funny thing happened on the way to prison for each one of these individuals. Each one was looking for a way to create some way to meet the need of control and then believe that they had certainty. And you know what? They each achieved it. Each has the absolute certainty that they will have a place to stay tonight. They have absolute certainty they have a blanket to lie under. They have absolute certainty they will have food to eat. And they have absolute certainty that they would absolutely change places with you today. The vehicles (behaviors) that we choose in reality are the choices we make. Choices create control. Choose wisely.

CHAPTER TWO
Variety

"There is no greatness without a passion to be great."

—Anthony Robbins

Secrets about Variety: The Spice of Life

Of all the things men and women describe as the most difficult part of their incarceration, it is the need for variety. In our lives we experience a paradox between the two needs of Control and Variety. Just when we think we have full control of our life, the need for variety creeps inside our mind; and we must do something to relieve that need. When we don't, we feel uncomfortable and unfulfilled. Luckily, there are endless possibilities to experience the need of Variety in an accountable manner.

The letters and notes from within the prison walls have given us an extraordinary gift. The gift of allowing us, the reader, to experience their methods of experiencing the need of Variety. These writers describe which behavior they chose to experience Variety and in the end, how those choices created a destiny. Readers, begin to notice the vehicle (behavior) that is used. Is it a bicycle or is it a Mercedes'? You are about to discover that the means for experiencing Variety may come with a high cost.

The letters provided offer several examples that the authors used to meet their need for variety through negative vehicles. Some of them include: using drugs, experiencing multiple sex partners, driving fast in a car, driving while high, risking your life on a dare, committing petty crimes like shoplifting, or becoming a member of a gang.

On the other side, there are ways to get variety in a very unique and positive way. Have you ever thought about the thrill of variety when you learn something new? Experiencing something that stretches you and gives you so much stimulation because you have learned something new? How about variety when you take care of your physical body? How about getting a job and learning a new skill? How about going to see a new movie?

Variety is a true need. If you don't fulfill it in a powerful, positive way, you will unconsciously go to a place and take unconscious risks that you shouldn't.

So, let's see what some of the secrets of these inmates will give us. The secret insights they give us may be ones we, perhaps, had not thought of as secrets.

Letter from Kimberly

Kimberly

Never in a million years would I have imagined being in Federal Prison. I came from a loving home, good education, and a solid life, but I let the longing of love from a man influence every aspect of my life. I allowed the man I loved, my sons father, bring me into a world I thought was intriguing! Something like the Mafa movies you see on TV but with Arabs. This was a world of secrecy, money, fun, & danger. I so wish I could turn back the hands of time. My elders always said, "What decisions we make today will effect our lives forever!" And the Lord says, "The sins of the parent fall upon the children!" So at the time, I thought I was only effecting myself, & I thought "I'll never get caught!" But now, I've gone through 3 years of Hell. April 15, 2003, 32 DEA agents stormed my house w/assault weapons drawn, and my 4 year old sons was woken to this chaos. My life was on hold w/emotions running wild for 2½ years. Finally, I was sentenced to 37 months Federal Prison Time 85% must be served, but now my 2 boys are separated from me, My 60 & 64 year old parents are having to care for my boys, but just last month, the father of my youngest son came & took my 2 year old baby away from all he has known as family. My oldest sons father will be in prison for 20+ years! So listen to my plea! Run from the danger! Stay simple & keep to those who really care for you, not those that want to use you. What you do now will effect your life forever

35

Dear young lady,

Never in a million years would I have imagined being in a Federal Prison. I came from a loving home, good education, and a solid life, but I let the longing of the love that was different influence every aspect of my life. I allowed the man I loved, my son's father, bring me into a world I thought was intriguing! Something like the Mafia movies you see on TV but with Arabs. This was a world of secrecy, money, fun and danger. I so wish I could turn back the hands of time. My elders always said, "What decisions we make today will effect our lives forever!" And the Lord says, "The sins of the parent fall upon the children." So at the time, I thought I was the only one at risk. The risk would only affect me and I thought, "I'll never get caught." But now, I've gone through 3 years of Hell. April 15, 2003, 32 DEA agents stormed my house with assault weapons drawn, and my sons were awoken to this chaos. My life was on hold with emotions running wild for 2 1/2 years. Finally, I was sentenced to 37 months Federal Prison Time, 85% must be served, but now my 2 boys are separated from me, my 60 & 64 year old parents are having to come for my boys, but just last month the father of my youngest son came and took my 2 year old baby away from all he has known as family. My oldest son's father will be in prison for 20+ years. So listen to my plea! Run from the call that pulls at you. Stay simple and keep to those who really care for you, not those that want to use you. What you do today will effect your life forever.

Kimberly,
Federal Correctional Institution, Marianna, Florida

What is Kimberly's secret and message to you?

Kimberly reaches out to tell you that her extreme need for something different and exciting drove her to make choices that created a life that placed her into your path today. You cannot imagine how many times I have heard her story repeated, "(I went) into a world I thought was intriguing!" Kimberly's words, "Finally, (when) I was sentenced." ring out loud and clear. Only when absolute certainty returned did she begin the journey of putting her life back into some resemblance of order.

What did you take from this message? What will you do in your future to create Variety?

_____

_____

_____

Letter from Alejandra

Hey You!   8-29-06

I was one of you when I came to prison.
I had just turned 17. You are surely doing
some, if not all of the things I was doing
at that time in my life. I was in high
school, I had a job, a car, and tons of
friends. I was responsible in many ways
but I also did my share of partying. I
drank a little, smoked a little pot, dropped a few hits of LSD. No big deal, right?
Yeah, that's what I thought too. To make a
long story short, one night, while going to
buy some weed, a guy that was with me
killed the pot dealer and the pot dealer's girlfriend. I drove him to and from the apartment to buy the pot. Something as innocent
as smoking a little weed turned into a
double murder. The killer got two life
sentences and so did I, as a "party to
the crime". I was 17, a teenager, a kid,
just like you, just like your friends. I'm
now 31, a convicted murderer is the label
I carry, and I have 15 years in prison
under my belt. Don't end up like me. Stay
far away from drugs. I wasn't a drug
addict and you may not be one either, but
drugs, even dabbling with them always
leads to destruction. I have yet to meet a

38

person, out of the thousands I've met throughout the years, whose reason for being in prison is not somehow related to drugs. Drugs may not be your addiction, as it wasn't mine but they will lead you to be around drug dealers, guns, violence, drug addicts, and situations as innocent as mine that could land you in prison for the rest of your life.

With Love,
Alejandra

Hey You,

I was one of you when I came to prison. I had just turned 17. You are surely doing some of it, if not all of the things I was doing at that time in my life. I was getting high in high school; I had a job, a car, and tons of friends. I was responsible in many ways but I also did my share of partying. I drank a little, smoked a little pot, dropped a few bits of LSD. No big deal, right? Yeah, that's what I thought too. To make a long story short, one night, while going to buy some weed, a guy that was with me killed the pot dealer and the pot dealer's girlfriend. I drove him to and from the apartment to buy the pot. Something as innocent as smoking a little weed turned into a double murder. The killer got two life sentences and so did I, as a "party to the crime." I was 17, a teenager, a kid just like you, just like your friends. I'm now 31, a convicted murderer is the label I carry, and I have 15 years in prison under my belt. Don't end up like me. Stay far away from drugs. I wasn't a drug addict and you may not be one either, but drugs, even dabbling with them always leads to destruction. I have yet to meet a person out of the thousands I've met through the years, whose reason for being in prison is not somehow related to drugs. Drugs may not be your addiction, as it wasn't mine, but they will lead you to be around drug dealers, guns, violence, drug addicts and situations as innocent as mine that could land you in prison for the rest of your life.

With love
Alejandra, Alto State Prison, Georgia

What is Alejandra's secret and message to you?

"Variety, the Spice of Life," this is such an enthralling statement. This need for something totally out of the ordinary that makes us feel life is now at its best. Alejandra describes how her innocent journey had tragic consequences for many in her life. She is absolutely right about her way of seeing how drugs affect individual's lives. You may crave the human need of variety and DRUGS will fill that need instantly. However, the power of drugs is far greater than any one of us can imagine. Alejandra simply begs each of us to find a better way to fulfill this need of variety. Drugs are not the answer for fulfilling this need.

What did you take from this message? What will you do in your future to create Variety?

_____

_____

_____

Letter from Jeffrey

To Any Young Adult.

My Story Is differant Than Most in The way That I had everything I didn't need to Sell drugs My family has o money. Their were Several Things That I did which enaBled me to destroy my Life. I Believe my worst flaw was I failed to plan. which equals planning to fail. Due To My Lack of Vision I never saw me doing the Right thing. So I never planned At The Age of 12 I was An Alcoholic And Drug Addict. I admired The older guys who didn't work But Sold drugs They had money, Homes, girels, cars, Jewelery, and Basically All they wanted. I wanted The Power They had. Plus I Thought It was Cool. I wanted to Be "Cool" Life Them. So I Become A worker For them. I missed school Stayed out All Night And Disrespected My family I pursued The Lifestyle Right into A Pennitentiary. Thats Basically my Story I don't want to Bore you with detoils I had People Preach to me my whole Life. It never worked I Been locked up 3 times As A Minor And Once in A Pennitentiary now. What Worked For me Is Coming to Jail And Realizing all The Pain I had caused my family And Those I Loved. If I culd Say whats The one Thing I wald have done differant now looking Back Thats simple Don't Do Drugs. Thats My #1 Peice of Advice which I Know you've heard 1 million Times BUT Its true. NExt wald be Listen To your Parents It Took me 23 years To Realize who my 2 Best Friends Are Thats my mom And Dad. Plan Plan Plan you Can do Anything you want to

42

You Can Be What you want to Be Follow your Dreams
don't Let Nothing or Nocne Stand IN Your way.
The Sad News Is That If you Are AnyThing At Like I
WAS Then All This Iam Telling you Doesn't Matter.
Like me you'll have to Learn Threw experience either The
Hard way or easy way Thats UP to you. Get A good
Roll Model Follow his Lead. Never give UP
on your Dreams. Life Is to Wonderful to Spend IN A
Drug induced Coma or to even waste 1 second IN
A Prison. Thats All I have. All I Told you was Told To
me 1 million Times I hope unlike me you Listen to
What I've Said. Remember Above All Plan. And Don't
Do Drugs. ever.
                    Good By And Good Luck.
Things I Should Have Learned.

To any young adult,

My story is different than most in the way that I had everything. I didn't need to sell drugs. My family has money. There were several things that I did which enabled me to destroy my life. I believe my worst plan was "I failed to plan," which equals "planning to fail." Due to my lack of vision I never saw me doing the right thing. So I never planned to do it. At the age of 12, I was an alcoholic and drug addict. I admired the older drug addicts. I admired the older guys who didn't work, but sold drugs and they had money, homes, girls, cars, jewelry, and basically all I wanted. I wanted to feel the thrill of it all and I thought it was cool. I wanted to be "cool" like them. So I became a worker for them. I missed school, stayed out at night, and disrespected my family. I pursued the lifestyle right into the penitentiary. That is basically my story. I don't want to bore you with details. I had people preach to me my whole life. It never worked. I've been locked up 3 times as a minor and in a penitentiary now. What worked for me is coming to jail and realizing all the pain I had caused my family and those I loved.

If I could say what the one thing I would have done different now looking back that is simple. Don't Do Drugs. That is my #1 piece of advice, which I know you've heard 1 million times. But it is true. Next, would be listening to your Parents. It took me 23 years to realize who my 2 best friends are that's my mom and dad. Plan, Plan, Plan you can do anything you want to. You can be what you want to be. Follow your dreams, don't let nothing or no one stand in your way. The sad news is that you won't believe me.

You will have to learn them through experience. You will learn either the hard way or easy way, that is up to you. Get a good role model, follow his lead. Never give up on your dreams. Life is too wonderful to spend in a drug induced coma or to even waste 1 second of life in prison. That is all I have. All I told you was told to me 1 million times. I hope, unlike me, you listen to what I've said. Remember above all, Plan. And don't do drugs, ever.
Good by and good luck,
Jeffrey

What is Jeffrey's secret and message to you?

Jeffrey warns us that seeking the need for variety with drug use will create definite consequences. Those consequences are described as "I failed to plan which equals planning to fail." Of course, we are all warned of this in life; we have all heard the warning before. You have got to see where you are going so you can get to where you want to go. For just a moment, move over to this side of the wall so you can see what is coming. That is his warning. The sad part is that he recognizes that you are, in fact, him and that he wishes to go back and plan. His journey has created an alliance that was unexpected in his life. He moved back towards the middle of the paradox between certainty and variety once he understood there were individuals waiting to help him plan for his life. Is it possible that real variety can come cloaked with the challenge of creating a plan for your life?

What did you take from this message? What will you do in your future to create Variety?

_____

_____

_____

Letter from DeWaymer

If you run with your homeboy's, neighborhood clicks or [16] even gangs, slow down. The homies ain't what they really seem. To live street fame, you will experience street pain or face death, either literally or mentally by doing drugs. Today I'm still in prison for being a gangbanger, I've did 13 years, facing the hardest time in all my life, being without my family, having different family members die and can't even go to the funeral. School is a valuable tool to survive in this world. Everything your homies offer your teacher can give you twice without ever being in here where I'm at right now, hurting because my son is without a father. I did drugs, smoking weed with my gang homies and committed murder, nobody from the gang ever wrote me, visited me or even sent me a picture! Was it worth it, no, it was stupid and it's stupid being in here because of gang violence and being in a gang. There's no life in prison, school is life, it don't make you fake to stay in school. Please listen!

DeWaymer

If you run with your homeboy's neighborhood clicks or even gangs, slow down. The homies ain't what they really seem. To live street fame you will experience street pain or face death, either literally or mentally by doing drugs. Today I'm still in prison for being a gangbanger, I've did 13 years, facing the hardest time in all my life, being without my family, having different family members die and can't even go to the funeral. School is a valuable tool to survive in this world. Everything your homies offer, your teacher can give you twice without ever being in here where I'm at right now, hurting because my son is without a father. I did drugs; smoking weed with my gang homies and committed murder, no body from the gang ever wrote me, visited me or even sent me a picture! Was it worth it? No, it was stupid and it's stupid being in here because of gang violence and being in a gang. There's no life in prison. School is life, it don't make you fake to stay in school. Please Listen!!!!!!!!

DeWaymer

What is DeWaymer's secret and message to you?

The need for variety can create unwanted fame. DeWaymer describes what really happens in life when the world of gang violence fills this need we call variety. He warns us to look at this part of his life. Look at what gangs have really given him when he used gang membership as the tool to fulfill his need for variety. I have often heard Tony describe individual's lives as shining brightly in one of two ways. You are either a beacon of possibility or a flashing warning light. Here we learn that seeking to fulfill the need of variety in a gang is a… Well, you be the judge.

What did you take from this message? What will you do in your future to create Variety?

_____

_____

_____

Letter from Jana

"Watch" what you're doing,
   "STOP" & think it through.
I've been there before,
   I once, was like you.
The drugs were fun
   The sex was fast.
I loved riding in fast cars,
   My foot heavy on the gas.

Now 3 children later,
   With 12 felonies to boot.

All those fun & games
   Aren't such a Hoot!
You ~~and~~ learn some hard lessons
   From behind these walls.
You find who your friends are,
   when they won't accept your calls.

That's right - collect calls only.
Now - who are you? Are you real or phony?
    Behind these walls,
        You'll see scenes untold.
Most will do anything for a Debbie Cake -
    Most will sell their souls.
This is one lesson
        I hope you'll never learn.
    But stop & think about it -
        Or else you'll get burned!

                    Jana

                    Aug - 2006
                    Metro State Prison
                    Atlanta, GA

49

"Watch" what you're doing, STOP and think it through. I've been there before. I once was like you. The drugs were fun. The sex was fast. I loved riding in the fast cars. My foot heavy on the gas. Now 3 children later with 12 felonies to boot. All those fun and games aren't such a hoot! You learn some hard lessons from behind these here walls. You find who your friends are, when they won't accept your calls. That's right—collect calls only. Now—who are you? Are you real or phony? Behind these walls. You'll see scenes untold. Most will do anything for a Debbie Cake. Most will sell their souls. This is one lesson I hope you'll never learn. But stop and think about it—or else you get burned.
Jana, Metro State Prison, Georgia

What is Jana's secret and message to you?

Jana describes variety as an experience that fulfilled her in the moment. However, in the long term, seeking the thrill that variety provides cost her greatly. She asks us for just the split second of a heart beat to consider what the outcome of the thrilling experience would be. Simply "STOP and think it through."

What did you take from this message? What will you do in your future to create Variety?

_____

_____

_____

50

Closing Thoughts

Variety is always going to be with us. Variety is actually one of the essential parts to feeling like we have a life worth living. How you choose to fulfill this need is really the key to happiness. You've seen many examples of ways that variety has created pain. As there are many ways to create pain with variety, there are even more ways to create variety in ways that are powerful and loving that will enhance the quality of your life. Yes, it will always be there, the need for variety.

The balance between the needs of Control and Variety is a powerful paradox. If I have too much control, I need to go over and experience variety. When I have too much variety, I have to stop the madness, go back and get some control. It's always a delicate balance in life. The key through it all is learning which vehicle (type of behavior) provides you the most powerful way to enjoy your life at its fullest.

CHAPTER THREE
Significance

"All emotions are pure which gather you and lift you up. That emotion is impure which seizes only one side of your being and so distorts you."

—Rainer Maria Rilke

"The quality of your life will always be reflected by the expectations of your peer group."

—Tony Robbins

Secrets about Significance

Of all the human needs, this is usually the one that is easiest to identify. The behavior, again, is a vehicle to fulfill the need that you seek to experience. That behavior can range from anywhere between a bicycle to a racecar. The need for significance is a continuing human event.

Understanding that we are all driven to find some way to meet this need in a manner that enriches our lives is the secret to really feeling happy and fulfilled. Significance gives me purpose of life, creates a feeling that I'm needed. It's a special way of saying that I am really unique. I am something special. I'm beyond what the average person is. I get a feeling of importance.

Significance is often gained by using nothing more than a title. Some of the writers will describe their title and the price they paid for that title. Some will describe how they gained significance by instilling fear in others with their own powerful anger. Many gained importance by becoming a gang member, acquiring a bad reputation, skipping school, using intimidation, fighting, causing confusion. All of these vehicles (behaviors) made that individual at that precise moment feel significant. However, was it the best vehicle to use to gain their significance?

Let's look at some powerful positive behaviors that meet the need of significance in style. Mastering a skill, doing the right thing when there is a challenge, being of service to another human being, and educating yourself, are all positive vehicles to significance. Just the letters Ph.D create a totally unique individual. Inside each of us is the secret desire to feel that our efforts are being appreciated, that our presence on this planet is valued and appreciated, and that somehow, just because I was here, someone's life was touched. That's what significance truly means. The following messages will help you identify what kind of vehicles these writers used to meet this need called significance.

Letter from Carla

Po Box 109/ E-1/119
Alto, Ga 30510   8/29/06

Hey Whatz 1?

My name is Carla & I'm writing you this letter in hopes that it'll help turn your life around.

I'm currently in prison for Criminal attempt burglary, V&CSA, & forgery 1st degree. Whatz really happening is I tried to pull a caper to buy more crack & gave the po-po all AKA Name.

What I'm trying to say is everybody got a story to tell & it sounds sensational, but it really boils down to ~~making~~ Making some stupid decisions.

In my hood it sounds cool to say "yeah I just did a bit" or "I'm a hustler". But for real thuggin leads to nothing but jails, institutions or death.

So that thug who's really a "busta" that's tradin war stories w/others

55

2) is really sensationalizing his Rap. He aint telling you about how he was snorting & had a habit; had went crazy; or he aint telling you how he done broke his mother's heart, or how aint nobody from them streets wrote or sent him one dime; or how ~~niggaz~~ them others done made him a punk cause he want some zoom zoom & wham whams, or how aint nobody accepting his phone calls; or how he has no where to parole out to. Silently at night he ~~cry~~ cries & wishes he woulda done things differently or listened to somebody; ~~Him~~ His mom, grandmother or preacher at church & guess what? Don't let it be too late - I never seen a man cry until I seen a man die & it don't have to be a physical death - spiritually you can die inside.

So please stop & turn & be true to the game by not ~~using~~ playing the game & start New.

with much love

Evangelist Carla

Lee Arrendale State Prison
Alto GA

56

Hey Whatz,

My name is Carla & I'm writing you this letter in hopes that it'll help turn your life around. I'm currently in prison for criminal attempt burglary, VOCSA & forgery 1st degree. Whatz really happenin is I tried to pull a caper to buy more crack & gave the po-po an AKA name. What I'm trying to say is everybody got a story to tell & it sounds sensational, but it really boils down to making some stupid decisions. In my hood it sounds cool to say "Yeah I just did a bit U. I'm a hustler. But of real thuggin leads to nothing but jails, institutions or death. So this who's really a bustin that's trading war stories w/others is really sensationalizing his RAP. He ain't telling you about how he was snorting & had a habit & had almost went crazy. Or he ain't telling you how he done broke his mothers' heart, or how ain't nobody for them streets wrote or sent him one dime, or how them others done made him a punk cause he want some zoom zoom & Wham Wham. Or how ain't nobody accepting his phone calls or how he has nowhere to parole out to. Silently at night he cries & wishes he would done things differently or listened to somebody. His mom, grandmother or preacher at church & guess what? Don't let it be too late— I never seen a man cry until I seen a man die & it don't have to be a physical death—spiritually you can die inside. So please stop and turn & be true to the game by not playing the game.

With much Love,
Carla, Lee Arrendale State Prison

What is Carla's secret and message to you?

Carla's "secret" message is tell you that those who boast about what they have achieved in a negative way are simply looking for a way to elevate how they see themselves. Notice how she tells us that when they are alone at night that they cry in the darkness. They feel so badly about themselves that they will do virtually anything in the moment to feel like they are important to someone. Knowing that you are without value to anyone in life and that no one will even write you or accept a call from you is total insignificance. This path she warns will lead to a physical death or you will spiritually die inside. Her secret for staying out of prison is simply, "...stop and turn and be true to the game by not playing the game."

What did you take from this message? How could you live your life by making someone else feel Significant?

Letter from Brian

Stay Out of TRouble
G to school and MaKe
youR motheR pRoud
And don't be liKe Me

BRian

Marriott J.V. Center
Apr 13

Stay out of Trouble.
Go to School and make your mother proud.
And don't be like me.

Brian, Age 13
Marietta, J.V. Center

What is Brian's secret and message to you?

Brian's message is simple and powerful. He instinctively knows that there is no greater way to achieve significance in his life than to make his mother proud. His message is to not be like him, but to do something that will make your mother PROUD!

What did you take from this message? How could you live your life by making someone else feel Significant?

_____

_____

_____

Letter from Terry

Greetings,

I'm writing this from prison. I've been locked up for 8 years. It dosen't matter what my charges are. What I want you to know is that I've been locked up because I gave into peer presure. I wanted every one to think I was cool and tuff. I wanted every one to know I wouldn't take crap off any one. Well, since I've been in prison I've had to take alot of crap. Not from the inmates, But, from the staff. My point is you don't have to prove who you are or any thing like that. Your true friends will respect you no matter what. Don't worry about what your "So called friends" think. And believe me you have more so called friends than you think.
   So just be yourself.

Your Friend

Terry

Greetings,

I'm writing this from prison. I've been locked up for 8 years. It doesn't matter what my charges are. What I want you to know is that I've been locked up because I gave into peer pressure. I wanted everyone to think I was cool and Tuff. I wanted everyone to know I wouldn't take crap off anyone. Well, since I've been in prison I've had to take a lot of crap. Not from the inmates, but from the staff. My point is you don't have to prove who you are or anything like that. Your true friends will respect you no matter what. Don't worry about what your "so called friends" think. And believe me you have more so called friends than you think.
So just be yourself.
Your friend,
Terry, Federal Correctional Institution, Marianna, Florida

What is Terry's secret and message to you?

Terry's message is that the illusion of being "tuff" is not the best way to experience significance. Living your life at a level where you must act the part of being "tuff" and intimidate others will ultimately cost you. His secret, "Don't worry about what your 'So called friends' think." Your true significance comes when you become truly aware of how much you can achieve.

What did you take from this message? How could you live your life by making someone else feel Significant?

_____

_____

_____

Letter from Ciscero

My NAME IS CISCERO

I'm A 27 yr. OLD AFRICAN MALE. I'VE BEEN INCARCE-
RATED NOW OVER 12 yrs AND ARE STILL COUNTING. I WAS ONCE YOUR
AGE AND MY MISSTAKE WAS THAT I DIDN'T REALLY VALUE LIFE.
ALL OF MY FRIENDS WAS CLASS CLOWN, "THE ONE WHO ALWAYS
SKIP AND CUT UP IN SCHOOL." I CAME FROM A HOUSE HOLD OF DESC.
ENT FAMILY MEMBERS, BUT THEY WASN'T ENOUGH TO STRAY ME
AWAY FROM MY BAD COMPANY I LOVED TO HANG OUT WITH.
I WRITE YOU THIS LETTER WITH SINCERITY. PLEASE, DO ONE THING
FOR ME. TAKE A SECOND TO REVIEW LIFE, SEE THE MANY BLESS
INGS THAT GOD HAVE GIVEN US IN HIS CREATION. REVIEW YOUR
FRIENDS, SO THAT YOU WILL NOT END UP IN THE SITUATION
I ENDED UP IN. ALWAYS LOVE AND PLACE NO ONE OVER
YOUR FAMILY. STAY AWAY FROM CRIMES AND RECIEVE YOUR EDUCA.
TION. PERSUE, ALL POSSIBILITIES AND SET OUT PERSONAL GOAL
THAT ONE DAY YOU SHOULD ACCOMPLISH.

SINCERITY YOURS

FRIEND

I'm a 27 yr. Old African Male. I've been incarcerated now for over 12 years and am still counting. I was once your age and my mistake was that I didn't really value life. To all of my friends, I was class clown, "The one who always Skip and cut up in school." I came from a household of decent family members, but they wasn't enough to stray me away from my bad company. I loved to hang out with. I write you this letter with sincerity. Please, do one thing for me. Take a second to review life, see the many blessing that God have given us in his creation. Review your friends, so that you will not end up in the situation I ended up in. Always love and place no one over your family. Stay away from crimes and receive your education. Pursue all possibilities and set out personal goals that one day you should accomplish.

Sincerity Yours Friend
Ciscero

What is Ciscero's secret and message to you?

Can Ciscero's "Secret" be what you need today? He asks you to review life today and make it important (significant). You are a gift to this world. Go and take a look at what you have. He has come to a firm resolution that having a family is truly unique and powerful. He asks you to make the family in your life a "significant experience." Make your goals significant enough to create accomplishments. These are his "secrets" for staying out of prison.

What did you take from this message? What will you do in your future to create Significance?

_____

_____

_____

Letter from T

Stay in school, and lear as much as you possibly can. You me, and others that has made several mistakes as a stepping stone. I am currently serving a 30 year sentence for distribution, and there isn't a day that I dont wake up, that I wish someone, anyone would've took just a minute of their most precious time to talk to me about straightening my life out. Whoever you're, please listen, and learn. Dont be in a rush to grow up, and work hard to get the things you desire, because if anything comes to you easy, there will most certainly be consiquences behind the action you took to receive whatever it was. The reaction could be good or bad, so be careful, and always pro-act before you react.

"T"

Stay in school, and learn as much as you possibly can. You me, and others that has made several mistakes as a stepping stone. I am currently serving a 30 year sentence for distribution, and there isn't a day that I don't wake up, that I wish someone, anyone, would've took just a minute of their most precious time to talk to me about straightening my life out. Whoever you're, please listen, and learn. Don't be in a rush to grow up, and work hard to get the things you desire, because if anything comes to you easy, there will be most certainly consequences behind the action you took to receive whatever it was. The reaction could be good or bad, so be careful and pro-act before you react.

T.

What is T's secret and message to you?

T's message is piercing about significance cloaked in a tool often referred to as wisdom. Having someone in your life to look up to is a key to staying out of prison… T. knows that he felt insignificant. He wanted to feel important to someone, somehow. He offers you his wisdom in this way: If you are not feeling important, go and talk to someone and make the other person feel important. He offers you the possibility of slowing down the events of life and taking the time to grow up and taking pride in the things you work to achieve. He offers an insightful thought—there is no easy way to achieve significance that matters. With too much ease comes a consequence.

What did you take from this message? What will you do in your future to create Significance?

_____

_____

_____

66

Closing Thoughts

Significance comes to us by the actions we take. Significance came to these men and women by behaving in ways that got the world's attention. They fulfilled their need for significance by "special" activities like: skipping school (they notice me now); using drugs (now they will see who is boss); instilling fear in others with their own anger (now see who is on top). Each of these vehicles created a level of significance in their lives, but at what price?

Their "secret" is to use the lessons they learned:

- Make family more important than yourself
- Be aware of your possibilities
- "Tuff" guys make "tuff" choices
- Anything worth learning is difficult
- Friends should be chosen wisely and reflect where you are going in life
- Make someone proud of you
- Be true to life itself; it's not just a game

How do you meet your need for significance? What vehicle (behavior) are you using to meet your need for significance? Is there a better way?

CHAPTER FOUR
Love and Connection

"People say that what we are all seeking is a meaning for life, I don't think that's what we are seeking. I think what we are seeking is an experience of being alive, so that our life experience on the purely physical plane will have residence with our own innermost being and reality.
What we actually feel is a rapture of being alive."

—Joseph Campbell

Secrets about Love & Connection

The Human Need of Love and Connection includes: a sense of bonding; experiencing intimacy; feeling a part of something; a sense of belonging; a oneness with self; a sense of sharing. These are all levels of love and connection. Everyone has the inner desire to be loved. This inner drive that we are all born with, often compels us to do things that may seem strange or unusual to someone else. There are individuals who outwardly express that they hate everyone in this life. Yet, these same individuals still have the inner need to feel that they are loved and connected to someone or something.

The desire to experience unconditional love, to experience the feeling of being valued by others, and to express unconditional love in return is one of the most powerful human needs. This driving need creates a place where you will want to feel like you are part of humanity. Living our lives with this feeling of love and connection adds a special quality to each of our lives. Love and Connection enriches everything we touch and creates a place of beauty that may otherwise go unnoticed.

If you have never experienced being loved and have no references for someone loving you, then you will feel like a vacuum cleaner has sucked out your soul. If you have ever been around anyone that has no love in their life, you truly feel sorry for them. This emptiness results in a feeling that plays out in their life by proving to the entire world why they are unworthy of love.

They eventually lash out at the world with behavior that creates pain for all those they touch.

The following messages will help you identify the kind of vehicles that are really available to meet this need for love and connection. What secrets do you think you're going to find?

Letter from Danica

8-18-06

Dear Friend,

I just want to inform you, that Being in Prison, is one of the most lonely time in my life. I often wished that I had taken the time out before I made this life changing mistake. Just a split second to think makes all the difference. I was not Connected with the Father above and so the Devil had Control of my mind, because I didn't take Control of my thoughts. You have to take your thoughts Captive, because your thoughts are the Road way that the Devil uses to get into your life.

Please listen to someone thats leading you in the right direction, don't always try to make your own Foot Prints in the Sand, learn from someone elses mistake. Be Bless! And Prayed up!

Always In Christ!
Danica

Dear Friend,

I just want to inform you, that being in Prison, is one of the most lonely times in my life. I often wished that I had taken the time out before I made this life-changing mistake. Just a split second to think, makes all the difference. I was not connected with the Father above and so the Devil had control of my mind, because I did not take control of my thoughts. You have to take your thoughts to captive, because your thoughts are the roadway that the devil uses to get into your life. Please listen to someone that's leading you in the right direction, don't always try to make your own Foot Prints in the Sand, learn from someone else's mistakes.

Be blessed and prayed up!

Danica

What is Danica's secret and message to you?

The road to connection has lots of simple little narrow paths for you to walk upon, offers Danica. She warns of the loneliness of a prison cell and tells us it is the worst pain she has ever experienced. The pain of having no one to love and having no one loving her is beyond what most of us can understand. I almost find this a paradox unto itself. You see, in prison there are people everywhere. The staff and other inmates are always watching you and are right beside you. You are never more than a few feet away from someone. All of these individuals surround you and still Danica experiences the powerful feeling of not being loved, the pain of loneliness. Only when a spiritual path is offered as a way to love and connect, is love felt and comfort experienced. The "Secret" here is for you to know that you are not alone, even when you believe you are alone. There is something greater than ourselves that loves you.

What did you take from this message? What will you do in your future to create Love and Connection?

_____

_____

❀Love Yourself❀

Precious young lady, this is the most important lesson I've ever learned, "Love yourself". I always thought I truely loved myself. I took care of myself, beautified myself, and got an education, but I realized later that I didn't truely love myself. If I would've truely loved my myself, I won't have got involved with anyone who didn't understand my true value. You are more valuable, than your realize. Please never lower your standards. All women have the tendancy to put others before them, because we are nuturers. But in order to love them properly we must love ourselves. That means never do anything that put our-selves in harm's way. Never com-pnses your beliefs or standards for someone else. Believe in yourself and never let anyone tear you down. Always feed yourself positively. Avoid any and all negativity. And alway remember you're the most valuable, precious being on this earth. You'll special, one of a kind. You're my future, so please always remember to "Live yourself".

Sincerely,
LING

Love yourself,

Precious young lady, this is the most important lesson I've ever learned, "love yourself." I always thought I truly loved myself. I took care of myself, beautified myself, and got an education, but I realized later that I didn't truly love myself. If I would've merely loved myself, I wouldn't have got involved with anyone who didn't understand my true value. You are more valuable than you realize. Please never lower your standards. All women have the tendency to put others before them, because we are nurturers. But in order to love them properly we must love ourselves. That means never do anything that puts ourselves in harms way. Never compromise your beliefs or standards for someone else. Believe in yourself and never let anyone tear you down. Always feed yourself positively. Avoid any and all negativity. And always remember you're the most valuable, precious being on this earth. You're special, one of a kind. You're my future, so please always remember to "Love yourself."
Sincerely,
Love

What is the secret and message to you?

This writer believes the "Secret" to love is to first love yourself. The simple act of loving yourself creates an internal value for you. She advises you to never lower your standards for anyone. To get the best from life, raise your standards. I can almost feel her plea for you to begin to value yourself more. She begs the readers not take risks that could result in consequences that you cannot even to begin to imagine. This writer is pleading with you to understand that you are one of a kind in this life, a true precious gem. She also envisions you as the future. She knows without a doubt that our future begins with this reader.

What did you take from this message? What will you do in your future to create Love and Connection?

_____

_____

Letter from Judson

To the future;

My name is Judson, and this is my 3rd
time in prison.

I was raised in a single parent home with a mother
struggling to work two jobs to provide for my sister
and I... In my Mothers flustration about her situation
in life being a teen mother; I recieved several beatings
for some things I deserved, and most just because she
wanted to let out her rage. I felt alone, and that no one
cared about what happen to me. I started living in
a fantasy world to forget about home and what we didn't
have. I wasn't focused on school and dropped out. I
was a runaway, thinking it would solve my problems. I
felt I didn't have a childhood, so I chose to be grown
early. I had my first child at 15 yrs old, and that
same year I joined a gang. I finally felt that I
had a family who loved me, so I did everything for
them I could, even neglecting my own responsibility
as a father. My life at a young revolved around
being what ever my gang needed me to, which I missed
out on doing things for me. I did the drugs, which
lead me not to think clearly. I sold drugs to survive
the streets at a young. And I continued to have
unprotected sex with girls, taking a chance on making
another baby, when I wasn't even taking care of my first
one. My point is, when things are hard, don't be afraid
to ask for help, cause alone you can get sucked up
into more problems. The choices you make at a young age
will affect your future adult life...

To the Future;

My name is Judson, and this is my 3rd time in prison. I was raised in a single parent home with a mother struggling to work two jobs to provide for my sister and I. In my mothers frustration about her situation in life being a teen mother, I received several beatings for some things I deserved and most just because she wanted to let out her rage. I felt alone, and that no one cared about what happened to me. I started living in a fantasy world to forget about how and who what we didn't have. I wasn't focused on school and dropped out. I was a runaway, thinking it would solve my problems. I felt I didn't have a childhood, so I chose to grow up early. I had my first child at 15 years old and that same year I joined a gang. I finally felt that I had a family who loved me, so I did everything for them I could, even neglecting my own responsibility as a father. My life as a youngster evolved around being what ever my gang needed me to do, which caused me to miss out on things for me. I did the drugs, which led me not to think clearly. And I continued to have unprotected sex with girls, taking a chance on making another baby, when I wasn't even taking care of my first one. My point is, when thing are hard, don't be afraid to ask for help, cause alone you can get sucked up into more problems. The choices you make at a young age will affect your future adult life…

What is Judson's secret and message to you?

Judson's "secret" desires are for you to think about how loving others and being loved affects your life in the long run. He writes about not feeling loved by his mother and the frustration she expressed that led to physical pain for him. Not feeling loved at home as a child led him to simply decide to grow up early. He began his search for love with gangs and tells us that this was not the answer either. Gangs demand loyalty but do not provide love. They provide an illusion of family but they never have that special love that families provide. He continues his search for love by fathering a child. But the gangs pulled him away, and he begins the cycle of not loving his own family. He continued his search for love with drugs, which only clouded his mind. His bottom line "secret" to the reader is to reach out, connect, and simply allow yourself to love. You cannot win this experience of life alone. A life without love will lead you to continually search for things that do not love.

What did you take from this message? What will you do in your future to create Love and Connection?

_____

_____

_____

Letter from Lisa

My name is Lisa and I'm a career felon. As I write this letter to you I think about how ignorant that I've been in how I transformed the plans that I had made for myself into a life of criminal activities. Loving money not myself or my children. Caring more for the high standards of the drug dealing lifestyle instead of the free productive lifestyle that I once had. I'm not an uneducated person. I have a degree and at one time goals to help the women that I live with, eat with and sit with while I write this letter to you. I say to you get the focus off of how you look in the eyes of the ones that's telling you to do those things that will bring you to unfortunate places such as prison's. I want to be what I use to be before prison. I cry sometimes because I miss who I use to be. Don't be a 49 year old wanting to do the things that you could've done at 25. Free without a record a prison record that is.

My name is Lisa and I'm a career felon. As I write this letter to you I think abut how ignorant that I've been in how I transformed the plans that I had made for myself into a life of criminal activities. Loving money not myself or my children. Caring more for the high standards of the drug dealing lifestyle instead of the free productive lifestyle that I once had. I'm not an uneducated person. I have a degree and at one time goals to help the women that I live with, eat with and sit with while I write this letter to you. I say to you get the focus off of how you look in the eyes of the ones that's telling you do those things that will bring you to unfortunate places such as prisons. I want to be what I used to be before Prison. I cry sometimes because I miss who I use to be. Don't be a 49 year old wanting to do the things that you could've done at 25. Free without a record a Prison Record that is.

What is Lisa's secret and message to you?

Lisa's message is one filled with a paradox. She experiences the powerful need of love and connection. However, she chooses objects that cannot love. They are simply things like money, lifestyle, and image. She is literally using a broken vehicle (behavior) to experience the need for love and connection. Her vehicle for experiencing love was slower than a bicycle and expensive as well. Her love and connection to a life in the fast lane took her on a path that has caused her immense pain. She tells us that love should include those who are closest to you. She says instead of looking into the eyes of those who would lead you to prison, look into the eyes of those you love and get truly connected to them.

What did you take from this message? What will you do in your future to create Love and Connection?

80

Letter from "C" (Oldest Inmate, in his 60s)

You,

I USED TO TAKE. SOMETIMES I USED TO HURT PEOPLE. ONE DAY CAME AND I TOOK SOMEONES LIFE. LET ME TELL YOU, THAT HURT A LOT OF PEOPLE REAL BAD. NOW, AFTER 15 YEARS I SEE WHAT I THOUGHT WAS EXCITING, FAST, AND FUN, AND STRONG...... IT WAS ONLY BEING SELFISH. WHEN YOU'RE SELFISH YOU ONLY TAKE FROM YOURSELF OVER AND OVER UNTIL IT HURTS SO MUCH BECAUSE YOU'RE ALL ALONE AND NOBODY THAT LOVES YOU CAN HELP ANYMORE. YOU CAN'T EVEN TAKE THIER HELP.

NOW I LEARN TO GIVE AND TO HEAL. I LEARN TO GROW. NOW IF ANYBODY HURTS ITS USUALLY AN ACCIDENT AND ONLY HURTS A LITTLE. NOW I HAVE LEARNED TO LOVE MOST EVERYBODY AND JUT CAUSE I HELP HEAL OTHER PEOPLE MAYBE I DON'T LIKE THEM BUT THE MAGIC THING IS I AM STILL GIVING INSTEAD OF TAKING.

AND WHEN I WAKE UP, I'm HAPPY ABOUT LIFE. NOT MINE - I MEAN HOW GREAT LIFE IS FOR EVERYBODY AND EVERYWHERE - AND THIS IS FOOD THAT KEEPS ME FEELING GOOD. IT MAKES ME SMILE.

I DIDN'T USED TO FEEL THIS GOOD. I THOUGHT I'D ALWAYS BE IN TROUBLE AND HURTING FAMILY, FRIENDS AND OTHER PEOPLE.

BUT TODAY I DON'T EVER HAVE TO THINK ABOUT IT AGAIN.

I KEEP MY EYES ON GOD AT ALL TIMES AND THE LESSONS JESUS TRIED TO TEACH US. I LOOK, I LISTEN AND I THINK FOR MY SELF OF OTHERS. THEN I REACH OUT WITH HEALING HANDS.

YOU KNOW WHAT BRINGS HEALING TO YOUR HANDS FIRST?

YOUR MIND.

USE YOUR MIND.

ILL SEE YOU THERE,

C.

You,

I used to take. Sometimes I used to hurt people. One day came and I took someone's life. Let me tell you that hurt a lot of people real bad. Now, after 15 years I see what I thought was exciting, fast and fun, and strong......It was only being selfish. When you're selfish you only take from yourself over and over until it hurts so much because you're all alone and nobody that loves you can help anymore. You can't even take their help. Now I learn to give and to heal. I learn to grow. Now if anybody hurts, it's usually an accident and only hurts a little. Now I have learned to love most everybody and just cause I help heal other people maybe I don't like them but the magic thing is I am still giving instead of taking. And when I wake up, I'm happy about life. Not Mine—I mean how great life is for everybody, and everywhere—and this is food that keeps me feeling good. It makes me smile.   I didn't used to feel this good. I thought I'd always be in trouble and hurting family, friends and other people. But today I don't ever have to think about it again. I keep my eyes on God at all times and the lessons Jesus tried to teach us. I look, I listen, and I think for myself of others. Then I reach out with HEALING HANDS.

You know what brings healing to your hands first?
Your Mind.
Use your mind.
I'll see you there.
C.

What is C's secret and message to you?

"C" gives you an insight to real joy and happiness in life. It's perhaps the best kept "secret" of all, simply reaching out with healing hands to others. Experiencing love requires your ability to simply give of yourself to others; because in prison you truly have nothing but yourself to give. When you give of yourself unconditionally, a new possibility of joy begins, as if by magic.

What did you take from this message? What will you do in your future to create Love and Connection?

Closing Thoughts

Love and connection is something that each of us needs every day of our life. These letters paint the image in our mind of what life would be like to use vehicles that destroy. They chose negative vehicles (behaviors) in order to experience this powerful human need we call love because they were looking for the easy way to achieve love and connection. Love and connection caused these writers to choose the vehicle of money, power, sex, and drugs. Yes, these vehicles met the need in the short term. Yet, each was left feeling alone and in a place that left a broken spirit, in a place called prison. Their secret to us is to use the lessons they've learned.

The lessons they provide us are:
- People are more loveable than things.
- Love someone and they will love you back.
- Drugs cannot provide love.
- Family is a true source of love.
- Connecting to God is a powerful source of connection and love.
- You can't love anyone unless you first love yourself.
- Living without love is true punishment and true pain.

Those are the secrets presented to you. How do you choose to find love?

CHAPTER FIVE
Growth and Development

"Anything we fail to reinforce will eventually dissipate."

—Anthony Robbins

The Secrets about Growth & Development

Everything in life is either growing or dying; it's a fact of life. The law of life is that everything must serve a purpose. The feeling that one has more to learn and to give is always with us, and that growing need must be fed.

The examples of the bicycle vehicles (behaviors) that are often used to get this experience of growth is playing a videogame, learning how not to learn, creating an identity that says "I can't learn," and not expressing or using one's talents.

Let's look at some rewarding ways to experience this need called Growth.
Learning something new in school, the joy of doing and creating, expressing and sharing what you've learned or experiencing life to the fullest are all part of the need for growth and development. This human need is often the determining factor of how you feel about life in the moment. Are you growing and becoming or dwindling and dying? There is no greater joy in life than knowing the joy of becoming and creating. We all have that secret desire and wonder, is there more in store for me to experience in life? This need helps fuel the yearning that gets us past the moments of discouragement and anxiety and creates a place where we actually build our self-worth. Growth truly becomes part of our journey.

Letter from Claudia

Page 1
2
∞

8/29/06 Claudia

Metro State P.
Atlanta GA

First and foremost I'd like to tell each and every one of you the 4/1 who are reading this letter that its very easy to get caught up in things that can cause you a life "With" a record. Also know that anyone is susceptable to being behind these walls. But and its a big 'But' you can come out a stronger, wiser, and far more educated than you came into a place like this. I have been incarcerated for over eleven (11) years now. First offence. I've turned a bad situation into a positive one. I've gotten my G.E.D., am prensently in my fourth year of A.S.L. (American Sign Language) and even taken a course in office skills which included using the computer, which I'd never even turned on prior to Prison.

So What I'm saying is stay out of a place

86

like this. Learn skills out there in the real world. If you think your parents are rough on you boy you don't know the half of it.
Things are done their way in here. You do Not and I repeat do Not have a voice behind these dreary prison walls.
No phone calls except after 4:00 p.m. Timed on the phone, drab brown uniforms. No lacy clothers or boxer shorts for the men. Packed over crowded rooms and over worked officiers bringing their problems from home in as they use us as scape goats.
Fairness? What is that. It just doesn't exist inside. The only thing that will remain yours is an education and skills. Do yourselves a favor don't go pass go are you will come to jail which leads to prison.

First and foremost I'd like to tell each and every one of you who are reading this letter that its very easy to get caught up in things that can cause you a life "with" a record. Also know that anyone is susceptible to being behind these walls. But, and it's a big But, you can come out stronger, wiser, and far more educated than you came into a place like this. I have been incarcerated for over eleven (11) years now. First offense. I've turned a bad situation into a positive one. I've gotten my G.E.D. and presently in my fourth year of A.S.L. (American Sign Language) and even taken a course in office skills which included using the computer which I had never turned on prior to prison. See what I am saying is stay out of a place like this. Learn skills out there in the real world. If you think your parents are rough on you boy you don't know the half of it. Things are done their way in here. You do not and I repeat do not have a voice behind these dreary prison walls. No phone calls except after 4:00 P.M. Timed on the phone, drab brown uniforms. No lacy clothes or boxer shorts for the men. Packed over crowded rooms and over worked officers bringing their problems from home in and they use us as scapegoats. Fairness? What is that? It just doesn't exist inside. The only thing that will remain yours is an education and skills. Do yourselves a favor don't go pass go or you will come to jail which leads to prison.

Claudia, Metro State Prison, Atlanta, Georgia

What is Claudia's secret and message to you?

Claudia offers us some insight to what really is yours in life and how easy it is to lose what you believe you have. Her "Secret" is that wisdom is the only thing that cannot be taken from you. Even when you make a mistake in life, the learning gained from those mistakes is yours and will forever be yours. Yes, setbacks may occur, but learning (wisdom) and education are things the world can never take from you. Claudia also offers insight that it's never too late to learn. Growing and learning will lift you like nothing else possible.

What did you take from this message? What will you do in your future to Grow and Learn?

Letter from Andres

Andres

Educate yourself, I am
When making decisions remember the people involved
and the consequences for those actions.
Don't be afraid of failure and learn from your
mistakes.
Treat others the same way you want to be treated.
Always help the people that are less fortunate

age 15

Educate yourself.

When making decisions remember the people involved and the consequences for those actions.

Don't be afraid of failure and learn from your mistakes.

Treat others the same way you want to be treated.

Always help the people that are less fortunate.

Andres

Age 15

What is Andre's secret and message to you?

Andres "Secret" is simple but the simplicity comes with a pinch of the wisdom gained from experience. He offers this thought, "Educate yourself." He is telling us it's your responsibility to grow and learn, not someone else's. In addition, he offers the experience that when growing and learning occurs, mistakes happen. Don't be fearful of a mistake because growing is part of learning. The most successful people in life are those that overcome the most mistakes.

What did you take from this message? What will you do in your future to Grow and Learn?

_____

_____

_____

Young man you really need to look at my life and do the absolute opposite. First education is top priority in your life. Without it your setting yourself up at an early stage for a life of hardship and despairaty. Set a goal in your life then you stick to it all through school. Then when you graduate high school you re-evaluate your goal, and re-access what you have decided that you want in college, then you go for what you really want to become. Because your occupation should be something you love and can't wait till the next day to go to work. That kind of happiness will open your doors to all kinds of of joys that you have worked so hard for. Yes its just that simple Education first then all else will fall into a beautiful place.

Young man you really need to look at my life and do the absolute opposite. First, education is top priority in your life. Without it your setting yourself up at an early stage for a life of hardship and despairity. Set a goal in your life then you stick to it all through school. Then when you graduate high school you reevaluate your goal and re-access what you have decided that you want in college, then you go for what you really want to become. Because your occupation should be something you love and can't wait till the next day to go to work. That kind of happiness will open your doors to all kinds of joy that you have worked so hard for. Yes! It's just that simple Education first then all else will fall into a beautiful place.

What is this letter's secret and message to you?

This writer offers himself up as an example for you to learn from. Look at his life in prison and do the exact opposite. He expands his "secret" informing you that by establishing an early pattern of learning and growing everything else in life will simply fall into place for you. His message is to begin to grow and learn early in life. Remember, your life can be a beacon of possibility, or as this young man, a flashing warning light.

What did you take from this message? What will you do in your future to Grow and Learn?

Letter from Seaton

My NAME IS SEATON.

Listen, I'm in prison Now wishing I could be free, wishing I could work and have bills and pay bills - wishing maybe that I could be a kid again so I could make better choices.

Listen, forget all the fun of partying and forget about being the popular kid in school. Those things only end with TROUBLE. Be the Nerd, be the smart one who stays at home and does homework. Be the one who ends up happy, and successful, and FREE.

I took freedom for granted. The thug life is bullshit. Stay free.

Seaton

My name is Seaton.

Listen, I'm in prison now wishing I could be Free, wishing I could work and have bills and pay bills—wishing maybe that I could be a kid again so I could make better choices. Listen, forget all the fun of partying and forget about being the popular kid in school. Those things only end with trouble. Be the Nerd, be the smart one who stays at home and does homework. Be the one who ends up happy, and successful and FREE. I took freedom for granted. The Thug life is bullshit. Stay Free.
Seaton, New York State Prison

What is Seaton's secret and message to you?

Seaton offers a rare "secret" to ponder. He offers the lesson that the opportunity to pay a bill is a gift. The opportunity to learn and grow in order to pay the bills of life is truly one of the great "secrets" of life. One of the most powerful messages I ever heard came from Tony Robbins when he offered this thought to me: "Your greatest difficulty will be someone else's greatest opportunity." Here, Seaton, alone in prison asks you, the reader, to consider how much more your life would be if you took the opportunity to grow and learn. Learn how to take care of yourself each day without coming to prison.

What did you take from this message? What will you do in your future to Grow and Learn?

_____

_____

_____

Letter from Jasper

Coming from a $37\frac{1}{2}$ old man in prison I would like to reach out to young children to tell them this is not the way to go or the place to be in life please stick to your roots get a good education listen to your parents respect others set goals in your life and acheive them give back to your community be responsiable and enjoy your life be a good role model for your kids if you have any. stay positive. don't put off tommorow what you can do today.

Es. Jaspere

8/18/06

Coming from a 37 1/2 year old man in prison I would like to reach out to young children to tell them this is not the way to go or the place to be in life please stick to your roots get a good education listen to your parents respect others set goals in your life and achieve them give back to your community be responsible. Enjoy your life be a good role model for your kids if you have any. Stay positive. Don't put off tomorrow what you can do today.

Jasper, Texas State Prison

What is Jasper's secret and message to you?

This writer asks you to look at a different place for your growth and learning. Not only is the "secret" held in a place of learning. His underlying message is that the real "secret" is found when you begin to grow and learn from your parents. He also suggests another possibility. That the real spice of life comes when we reach out and give back to humanity. That is the real root of all happiness. Growing is not always about learning something new. Rather it's about living your life so others learn from you. Become the role model. Your choices in life will determine if you are a beacon or a warning light. Jasper asks that you make the choice today: "Don't put off (until) tomorrow what you can do today."

What did you take from this message? What will you do in your future to Grow and Develop?

_____

_____

_____

Closing Thoughts

Growth and learning present itself in many forms. The secrets presented, clearly provide awareness into the many avenues used to experience growth and development. Growth does not stop unless you choose for it to stop. The moment you decide you have nothing more to learn is the moment you begin to die inside. Each of these writers pleads with you, the reader, to go beyond your current expectations of learning, and find more ways to experience the Need of Growth. The "secrets" offered here are to use the lessons the writers learned and so you do not experience their pain.

The authors offer us these thoughts.
- No matter where you are in life, you still have the opportunity to grow and learn.
- Life is not fair. But, growth and learning can even the odds.
- You will fail as you go. Failing is part of the growth process.
- There always is an opportunity to grow.
- Education and growth first and the rest of life will simply fall into place.
- Growth is experienced spiritually as well as intellectually.
- Learning and growing come from all those around you including your parents, your teachers, and clergy.
- And never be surprised at what you may learn from a child.

You see, even behind the "wall" growth and development can take place, but the questions are: "Where do you choose to do your learning?" and "What is your subject matter?"

CHAPTER SIX
Contribution

"Only those who have learned the power of sincere and selfless contribution experience life's deepest joy: true fulfillment."

—Anthony Robbins

Secrets about the Gift of Contribution

In the world behind walls and in places where secrets are kept, I have observed individuals doing their best to "contribute" incredibly painful experiences to the world around them. Their contribution is intended to hurt all of mankind. They come along riding on a bicycle that is broken. They ride slowly, spilling out hate, so they feel less despised. They are cunning, so when the world's eyes are upon them, they will not be seen for what they really are. They are wily, so that the world will experience a touch of variety for the day's activities, and they use force to direct fear and create control over their situation. They are deceitful, so that love can never be directed towards them. They seek to "contribute" each of these characteristics to society causing themselves and those around them pain and suffering.

Just for a moment, consider a better vehicle (behavior) for contribution, one that will take you to true fulfillment using a method that will be forever etched in your mind. Adding value to all of life outside our own is the secret. Life's secret treasure is held in contribution. Whatever need you are missing you can only find it when you give it away. If you are missing certainty in your life, give certainty to those around you by becoming trustworthy. If you need love, become loving. If you feel insignificant, find a means to make someone else significant in your life. The reality to all of the "secrets" given is this: create a powerful self-esteem or self-image, to make the world about you a better place just because you were placed there. You have the power to make a difference in an individual's life no matter where you are or what your circumstance may be. Your "Secret Mission" is to go and make this a better world because you can.

Letter from Bruce

My name is Bruce,

I am currently serving a life sentence. Having been incarceration since my 19th birthday, I've missed out on a lot in life. Now that I am 36, I reflect back to see where I went wrong. I think that the biggest mistake I've ever made was to not take getting an education serious. Please don't make that same mistake. I was told many times by as many people that the road that I was on would lead to destruction. That was proven to be true. We all have choices that we can make. It's up to you to do what's best for you. Forget about being hip & cool. The coolest and hippest person is the one who doesn't fall for peer pressure. Be a leader & not a follower and do what's best for you. I leave you with this;

No matter how you turn a square it will stand on it's on, but a circle will be out of control. You can stand by yourself or be out of control in your circle of friends. The choice is yours.

My name is Bruce,

I am currently serving a life sentence. Having been incarceration since my 19th birthday, I've missed out on a lot in life. Now that I am 36, I reflected back to see where I went wrong. I think that the biggest mistake I've ever made was to not take getting and taking an education serious. Please don't make that same mistake. I was told many times by many people that the road that I was on would lead to destruction. That was proven to be true. We all have choices that we can make. It's up to you to do what's best for you. Forget about being hip and cool. The coolest and hippest person is the one who doesn't fall for peer pressure. Be a leader and not a follower and do what's best for you. I leave you with this:

No matter how you turn a square it will stand on it's own, but a circle will be out of control. You can stand by yourself or be out of control in your circle of friends. The choice is yours.

Bruce, Florence, Arizona Correctional Facility

What is Bruce's secret and message to you?

Bruce has experienced some of the deepest pain possible to a man. Yet he finds that the only real way to begin his journey back is by understanding what really happened to his life. His "secret" is so powerful that I cannot help but know he will touch many. If you can grasp this one piece of wisdom Bruce places within your heart and mind, your life truly will never be the same. Bruce offers this, " ....a square will stand on its own" no matter which side it is placed on "but a circle will be out of control." Simply become a square is his "secret."

What did you take from this message? What pieces of wisdom or skills do you have to Contribute? How can you enrich our world?

There comes a time in this life
when you finally "git it." When in
the midst of our fears and insanity
you stop and a voice in your head cries
out.... "Enough." After a few minutes
of heart breaking sobs, you begin to
calm down and look at the world
through a new pair of eyes. You begin to
realize there aren't always fairtale
endings in life ... or beginings for that
matter. In the process a new serenity
is born.
     You learn to open up to a new & different
point of view & you begin reassessing &
redefining who you really are & what
you really stand for.
          You learn that honesty & integrity
are not outdated ideas of a lost

era, but a foundation upon which life must be built. You learn that anything in this life worth having is worth working for. More importantly you learn that in order to achieve success you need direction, discipline & diligence. You may also learn that it really is ok to ask for help and even to give it away

Petra

There comes a time in this life you finally "Get it." When in the midst of our fears and insanity you stop and a voice in your head cries out...ENOUGH! After a few minutes of heart-breaking sobs, you begin to calm down and look at the world through a new pair of eyes. You begin to realize there aren't always fairytale endings... or beginnings for that matter. In the process, a new serenity is born. You learn to open up to a new different point of view, and you begin reassessing and redefining who you really are and what you really stand for. You learn that honesty and integrity are not the outdated ideas of a lost era, but a foundation upon which life must be built. You learn that anything in this life worth having is worth working for. More importantly you learn that in order to achieve success you need direction, discipline, and diligence. You also learn that is really is okay to ask for help and to give it away.
Debra

What is Debra's secret and message to you?

Debra's journey took her to a place where she learned that in order to achieve success, contribution was the key factor. She experienced that once you are past the fears and tears, what is left is this need to begin anew. Beginning life anew is not like a storybook. Life has a much richer meaning. You begin with creating a place for honesty and integrity as a foundation. Most of all, Debra tells us to reach out because that act makes all the difference in the world.

What did you take from this message? What pieces of wisdom or skills do you have to Contribute? How can you enrich our world?

Hancock State Prison

My Name is Terry   I'm In Hancock State
Prison. I'm 52 yrs old. I Just would Like to
Say first off is to Respect your Parents. This
is a must at this Day and time. Also that your
Life is you. So Life is only what you make it.
We all have Choices In Life, and I pray that
you Choose The Right Path. See I will never
get out of here. I will Die here. But I
will never give up. I Just hate that it took
me to get "Life" In Prison to See the mistakes
that I have made. Now I pray that this Letter
finds its way Into Some one Life and to be
that Motivational Letter To you. You Can make
that Right Choice.   May God Bless
I was Raise In a
Christian Home. A Preacher's
Son. So its not where you   Terry
from. Its where your   and may heaven
going. Change Playmates   Smile upon you.
and Play Grounds.

105

My name is Terry. I'm in Hancock State Prison. I'm 52 years old. I just would like to say first off is to Respect your Parents. This is a must at this day and time. Also that your life is you. So Life is only what you make it. We all have choices in life, and I pray that you choose the right path. See I will never get out of here. I will Die here. But I will never give up. I just hate that it took me to get "life" in prison to see the mistakes that I have made. Now I pray that this letter finds its way in to someone's life and to be that motivational letter to you—You can make that right choice. I was raised in a Christian home. A preacher's son. So its not where you're from. It's where you're going. CHANGE PLAYMATES AND PLAYGROUNDS.

God Bless,
Terry and may heaven Smile upon you

What is Terry's secret and message to you?

Terry's special "secret" is more powerful than anything I could have written. He wanted to make sure that his lessons were not lost lessons. His life may be a flashing warning light but not a loss… I cannot help but to agree with Terry that the key to experiencing the Human Need of Contribution is to change where you play. If you're playing in a "playground" where it's a weakness to improve the quality of your life, then perhaps you should consider a change. Consider the change not for me but for yourself and do it before it's too late.

What did you take from this message? What pieces of wisdom or skills do you have to Contribute? How can you enrich our world?

_____

_____

_____

Letter from Marcus

LITTLE BROTHER,

LISTEN GOOD BECAUSE I LOVE YOU ALL, IN THIS LIFE WE MUST FIND WHAT'S IMPORTANT TO US, NOT WHAT WE THINK WE WANT, OR NOT WHAT PEOPLE THINK WE SHOULD HAVE. BUT WHAT REALLY MAKE US HAPPY AND OTHERS HAPPY. LIFE IS ABOUT LOVE, AND WITHOUT LOVE LIFE REALLY IS MEANLESS, LOVE MAKES YOU FEEL GOOD WHEN YOU ARE BROKE AND DON'T HAVE NOTHIN TO YOUR NAME. LOVE IS THE KEY TO TRUE HAPPINESS. YOU SEE ONCE YOU LOVE THYSELF YOU CAN LOVE OTHER AND WHEN YOU LOVE THYSELF, YOU'LL WANT TO KNOW MORE ABOUT YOURSELF (THY INNERSELF) AND ONCE YOU KNOW THYSELF YOU'LL KNOW THAT EVERYTHING YOU NEED EXISTS WITHIN THYSELF. AND THEN YOU CAN LOOK AT LIFE IN A NEW SET OF EYES, AND FEEL GOOD ABOUT JUST ~~LIVING~~ BECAUSE YOU OR BEING ABLE TO TALK TO THE YOUTH OR SOMEONE WHO NEEDS HELP. MONEY DON'T BRINGS YOU HAPPINESS, IT ONLY GET SOME OF THE THINGS YOU THINK YOU WANT FOR THAT MOMENT. AND THEN EVERYTHING GETS OLD. BUT LOVE NEVER GET OLD, COLD, OR HOT, IT STAYS WARM FOREVERMORE. TAKE CARE

Love Struggle

MARCUS

HANCOCK STATE PRISON
P.O. BOX 334
SPARTA GA, 31087

107

Little Brother,

Listen good because I love you all. In this life we must find what's important to us. Not what we think we want, or not what people think we should have. But what really makes us happy and others happy. Life is about love, and without love life really is meaningless. Love makes you Feel Good When You are Broke and Don't have Nothing to Your Name. Love is the key to true happiness. You see, once you love thyself, you can love others, and when you love thyself, you'll want to know more about yourself (thy inner self) and once you know thyself you'll know that everything you need exists within thyself. And then you can look at life in a new set of eyes, and feel good about just living or being able to talk to the youth, or someone who needs help. Money don't bring you happiness, it only gets some of the things you think you want for that moment. And then evertything gets old. But love never gets old, good, or not, it stays warm forevermore. Take care, Love the struggle.

Marcus

What is Marcus' secret and message to you?

In Marcus' simplicity he reaches out to tell us that by giving the most cherished item in life one finds true happiness. He has uncovered the "Secret" of contribution. Love thy neighbor, even those that are unloving. It's at that moment he finds that the "Secret" to having it all was always within him.

What did you take from this message? What pieces of wisdom or skills do you have to Contribute? How can you enrich our world?

_____

_____

_____

Letter from Joseph

This is for all of you young adult:

It is my desire & wish that you all allow me to interfare. Listen & listen carefully & completely. My name is Joseph ~~Busby~~ I am now serving a 30 yr sentence, I have been down now 10 yrs. And I do not wish for you to be here, nor take my place. If I had someone to talk to before, I wouldn't be here now. "First lesson": trouble is easy to get into, but hell to get out of. "Second lesson": follow your own mind & goals, never let someone else dictate your actions, cause in the end it you that will ~~reap~~ reap the reward, or its you that will suffer the consequences of the action that has been taken. I wish I had more time to explain even more to you. So let me hit something here & there. Pay attention: I followed the wrong crowd, I wanted what everyone else around me had, and I got all I wanted & then something I didn't want & need. Such as being lock-up in prison away from my family, away from my daughter, I missed over ten years of her life, She was 5 yrs old, when I left the street, & now she's beginning High School. I took life for granted, please never take life for granted. Life will pass you by, Life will run over you, if you dont ~~~~ make a change today, tomorrow is not promise to you. I know I'm rumbling right now, but I trying to cover alot on one page. Now I'll try & sit down & write a mini book or article & I'll try I pass it on to the necessary person, or persons. And maybe, just maybe I can touch one of you young life, before it to late. If no one told you

over ↓

today I love you. And keep on Praying.
remember to keep on   P. U. S. H.

P	U	S	H
r	n	o	a
a	t	m	p
y	i	e	p
	l	t	e
		h	n
		i	
		n	
		g	

This is for all of you young adults:

It is my desire and wish that you all allow me to interfere. Listen and listen carefully and completely. My name is Joseph. I am now serving a 30 year sentence, I have been down now 10 years and I do not wish for you to be here, nor take my place. If I had someone to talk to before, I wouldn't be here now. "First lesson:" trouble is easy to get into but hell to get out of. "Second lesson:" follow your own mind and goals, never let someone else dictate your actions, cause in the end it's you that will reap the reward, or it's you that will suffer the consequences of the action that has been taken. I wish I had more time to explain even more to you. So let me hit something here and there. Pay attention: I followed the wrong crowd, I wanted what everyone else around me had, and I got all I wanted and then something I didn't want and need. Such as being locked-up in prison away from my family, away from my daughter, I missed over ten years of her life. She was 5 years old, when I left the street and now she's beginning high school. I took life for granted, please never take life for granted. Life will pass you by. Life will run over you, if you don't make a change today, tomorrow is not promised to you. I know I'm rambling right now, but I'm trying to cover a lot on one page. Now I'll try and sit down and write a mini book or article and I'll try to pass it on to the necessary person or persons. And maybe, just maybe I can touch one of you young life, before it to late. If no one told you today, I love you. And keep Praying. Remember to keep on.

P.	U.	S.	H.
r	n	o	a
a	t	m	p
y	i	e	p
	l	t	e
		h	n
		I	s
		n	
		g	

What is Joseph's secret and message to you?

Joseph gave this letter to me in tears. His greatest wish was to somehow make a difference to some person in life. He finally understood the "secret" of contribution. His dream was to somehow simply touch you in a way that hopefully will alter your destiny. You see Joseph's "secret" is held in P.U.S.H. I know it's simple. It's true. This whole effort is to let you know people have gone before you and it has cost them their lives. They await you, but what they really want to do is to continue to uplift you and wave to you as you pass them by.

What did you take from this message? What pieces of wisdom or skills do you have to Contribute? How can you enrich our world?

_____

_____

_____

Closing Thoughts

Contribution is a key to feeling like your life has truly made a difference to mankind. Contribution allows us to discover where the spice of life is for each one of us. When these men and women reached out to you—the reader—you cannot imagine how incredibly powerful the experience was. To know that life has meaning is truly magical. The individuals who reached out from behind these walls of stone and razor wire for the first time filled their life-long dream. I thank you for giving them this opportunity.

The "secrets" are lessons provided to you by someone who wishes to enrich your life.
- Starting over is okay when you pass on the lessons.
- Encourage others to play in the "playground" of enrichment.
- Serve those you love.
- Make a difference in the smallest way. It always counts.

These lessons are the "secrets" to having life and living life fully.

CHAPTER SEVEN
Moving Forward

"It's Easier Done, Than it is Said."

–Unknown

The Next Step

The failures of custodial institutions for over a century and a half haunt us daily.
- The homeless person who embarrasses
- The mental patient who shocks
- The chronic offender who threatens
- The teenage delinquent who elicits both fear and pity

Each reflects our society's inability to deal with individuals that appear marginal members of our communities. There are some who say we routinely institutionalize a given percentage of our population in our society. We have responded over the past 40 years with repeated strategies that continue to fail and see nothing but more pain on the horizon.

In the late 1980's research shows America began incarcerating the largest number of prisoners and youth in our history as a result of legislation that was passed in November 1985. We chose to begin to quit attempting to rehabilitate individuals who had broken our laws. We simply built more prisons and placed them behind walls so that we would not have to admit to ourselves that there is a problem. Thus, what one cannot see, one cannot be responsible for, therefore, we cannot have a problem. Society chooses to lock them up behind the walls and forget they are even there.

Our misplaced reliance on institutions has served to sap our imagination and leaves us with this question: "How do I possibly influence another human being?" The need to influence individual's behavior directly and permanently to live within the lawful boundaries established by government is a direction accepted by our society. And it's always going to be prevalent. How do I help another human being? That simply becomes the question. In the ever-evolving world, institutions have become a widely used alternative to redirect and control the behavior of youth. Infrequently, redirecting these individuals into less restrictive environments is not even considered as an option. As we begin this journey into the 21st century, we must search for alternatives.

Many of the individuals can be redirected through technology, influence, and positive psychology. These technologies can rapidly aid in the prevention of undesirable youth behaviors. It's critical in that we develop suitable programs that support cognitive change for "at risk teens."

One of the most powerful tools available to us is the results from the positive use of language and imagination. Individuals who are either in gangs, have a cycle of criminal behavior, are in juvenile facilities or incarcerated, appear to resist projecting their ability to use their imagination beyond eight to twenty-four hours at a time. They simply can't imagine creating a better tomorrow, so they stay the same. When asked, "Where do you see yourselves the next year?" they repeatedly respond, (almost 100% of the time) either dead or still in prison. The perception they have tells us, "I have no tomorrow. I only have what I have now. So, why do anything differently?"

What's the next step? How can I make a difference? Collectively, we need to begin to use our imagination by asking better questions. We now ask, how can we control misspent behaviors that cause pain to society? Perhaps a better question would be, how can we inspire young offenders to move towards a direction that betters mankind?

The Anthony Robbins Foundation is a powerful example of how meeting individuals human needs can change the world. The Foundation has grown from touching a few people with baskets at Thanksgiving to millions of people being cared for each year; from working with difficult teens to powerful Leadership Camp for teens; from providing tapes and books to prisons to providing educational material to thousands. Together we can make a difference.

Can I make a difference? That becomes a really paramount question. Because, once you ask it, you can. Oftentimes, we may believe we cannot make a difference because "I'm not in a place that I can help. I can't touch a teen. I don't have the training, the money, or the time. In fact, I'm not even a mother or a father, how can I help with this problem. What can I do?"

My advice to you would be this: find organizations that make a difference, then support those organizations. Because when you choose not to be a part of the solution, the problem persists until it festers and spills over on you. Become a part of the solution. Support organizations that do make a difference because the gangs are there when you aren't. Support organizations like the Anthony Robbins Foundation that do go out and make a difference. One thing I know for sure is this, doing nothing is a choice.

If you'd like to make a donation, go to www.secretsfrombehindthewall.com and you can make a cash donation by clicking on the donation button. And for every donation over $20, you will receive a copy of the book, "Secrets From Behind the Wall." Every dollar this book earns and every donation given goes to producing a film that teaches positive psychology for the purpose of pre-release programs for correctional and juvenile facilities.

On November 08, 2006 Associated Press released these headlines:
1 in 136 U. S. Residents Behind Bars.
Between 2004 and 2005, jails grew by 1,000 inmates each week.

These numbers are disturbing and should prompt each of us to ask what can be done. Please help these individuals that have healed from their mistakes reach out and allow their lessons not to be a lost voice in a forest of misspent lives.

CHAPTER EIGHT
Just the Facts

"It's not about getting what you want; it's about experiencing what you really need by becoming more."

—Anthony Robbins

The First Day

You're placed in a bus when you leave the county jail. You're wearing a jumpsuit that's four sizes too big. You have restraints called handcuffs and leg irons. The leg chain is 24 inches to 30 inches depending on your size, placed firmly around your ankles. The officer pushes the handcuffs tight and I can hear the double click sound that says, "You're mine." The belly chain holds your hands to your waist and the leg irons control your steps — then they tell you to walk. But it hurts to push against the irons. Bone to steel. Steel wins. You are pushed forward, toward a bus with twenty-five or thirty others.

You can almost taste the fear, because it's thick. The guards look at you strangely and say, "You're going to have a great day, boy." For some reason you want to talk but the stillness of fear is more powerful. You don't want to say anything because your mouth is so dry. And, then, the bus leaves. It's been at least an hour and the ride seems like you are going into "forever."

And, all of a sudden, you see this huge wall with an enormous twenty foot fence in front... It's got razor wire and not just one row. You look at it and there are twenty rows of razor wire on the ground. There are dead animals as far as you can see beside the fence because they touched the hot wire. You wonder, "What the hell have I gotten myself into?"

There are four officers who surround the bus with shotguns, machine guns and pistols. And you wonder, "What the hell have I gotten myself into," again. I haven't got a gun. And, they welcome you. They don't say a word. They just look at you and say, "Get your ass off the bus, boy." And you walk down a ramp into a steel world that has got a sound that will resonate in your soul for the rest of your life. The officers pack twenty of you in a small cubicle they call a sally port. The packing of human to human makes you, for the first time, take a deep breath and you can smell the putrid smell of each other.

Once that exterior door is locked, the outside world becomes a distant reality and is gone in an instant. Now the interior cell door leading inside opens, and they tell you to walk in.

You are placed in a holding cell. Eventually, you hear your name called. The cell door opens and you waddle out in your irons. They take you to a corner and begin to take the irons off your body. There are people standing everywhere but you're the only inmate out at the moment. "Everyone gets this special treatment." The officer says it plainly, "Strip'em."
You look around and you say, "Where do I strip at?"
And they say, "right there." You can't help but wonder why here, why not in a booth, why here in front of everyone, even her. And, you begin to strip. Slowly.

As you undress, you realize how fragile you really are behind these walls. As you stand there in your nakedness in front of two or three officers looking at you, evaluating you, they say raise your arms, wiggle your fingers to make sure there is nothing hiding there, turn around, bend over. They ask you to grab hold of your cheeks and pull. Someone laughs. Sometimes, they snort. You feel alone.

The young girl behind the desk giggles. Your feet are cold with fear. They tell you to turn around and lift them, "boy." That's when you turn around and ask, "Lift what?" "You know. Lift them," the officer yells. And you do. The officer with the chewing tobacco says, "Skin her back, son." And you've never felt so much shame.

If that wasn't bad enough, when you get through this phase of the shake down they walk up to you and say, "Open your mouth. Stick your fingers in your mouth and run your finger between your gums and teeth." You think, they can't be asking me to do this. Finally, they give you some clothes. And perhaps for the first time in your life, the meaning of feeling grateful is experienced.

120

The officer motions you to the finger printing area. Your prints are placed on a piece of cardboard. You ask a question and the officer nods yes, "Can I make a phone call?" The whole room laughs at you.

"You've got to be kidding," the officer responds.

"Yes sir, I want to call my mom and tell her where I'm at." His only response was to tell you to wash your hands.

The officer asks, "Do you have anything in your possession?"

You say, "I don't have much, I have some money, I have a driver's license. I have some personal items."

He says, "Let's put them in the envelope here. Where do you want them mailed to?" You ask. "Well, can't I keep them?"

"No, son, you can't. You can't keep anything from the outside," the officer states matter of factly. "You are not allowed to keep anything."

"Well, can I keep my pocket comb, my hair needs combed," you say.

"You didn't hear my words, boy. You can't keep anything here," the officer says again. "You don't understand, I have my address book where my attorney is at," you say.

The officer gripped the desk and looked you in the eyes coldly and said, " If you can't memorize it, you don't need it, boy."

" You don't understand, sir. My mom is expecting a call," you plead.

" I don't really care. Put them in the tray and welcome to prison," he says.

You are taken out of Receiving and discharged toward the place that you will call home. You can see forever because the long hall seems to go off into the distance. The floors are shiny and you walk down a corridor with cells on both sides, and you hear the screaming, and the madness begins. There are some guys whistling at you, other guys hollering at you. And all are yelling, "What are you here for?"

Time now has a new meaning. There is no such thing as time. You're doing time. Time becomes a place that is no longer a major factor of life. You are always there, tomorrow is the same as today. Days are measured by getting through, not by being on time.

121

After what seems forever, someone comes to your cell and states, "I'm your counselor."

He appears to be a nice person and he starts the conversation off by saying, "Don't waste my time. This is my time and I have questions for you. You need to sign this first. This document tells you that I told you that, you can't take, keep anything, any assets, and who do you want me to notify if you get killed?"

The counselor asked a second time, "I need to know who want us to notify when you are killed or if you're injured. Who do we notify?"

You had never thought about that, who is important enough to let know that I have died. You never had that thought before. I have to tell someone.

"My mother," was your response.

Then, you have the thought, does anyone even care? Did I burn my bridges? You hope for somebody that might care. They don't have to come to pick your body up if you die in here. You can't answer the question. Fear takes hold and buries the question.

The counselor begins his spiel by saying, "I'm taking you to the newcomers range. I have but one piece of advice for you, son. You can't have anything. For God sake, you must understand, everything someone gives you here is for a reason. Take nothing, not even a toothbrush, because that is something you will have to pay for later. There is no free lunch here. Nothing is free. Everything has a price attached to it." You nod with understanding.

He continues with a flat, practiced, statement, "I will give you what you need until you get your own things here from the commissary. Here is your toothbrush, which is cut off in half. It's only two inches long. Here is a small tube of powder. We don't want tubes here. Here is a bar of soap that has been broken in half. A towel and a washrag. One extra pair of shorts, one extra pair of pants. This is 100% of your possessions. Do you understand this is all you can have?" You nod in agreement. And you walk to your cell house.

The sounds of your shoes on the floor echo and you realize how out of place you are. You realize how innocent you are. Not from the crime you committed. But, you're innocent of what's about to happen. And you're afraid. Fear has a scent predators can smell.

You sit on the edge of your bed in your cell, they shut the door and turn the key locking you inside. The counselor looks at you coldly and says, "Son something I would always tell the new, I can only give you one thing, a piece of information that will serve you, kid. And this is it. I want you to understand there is only two types of people in this prison. You're either a predator or you are the prey. Choose wisely." And your time has begun.

A large bell rings, a buzzer goes off. And your cell doors unlock and slide open. And it's the first time you are about to go to have a prison meal. Everybody goes at the same time, when they call your floor for mainline. And you go, and for the first time, you're going to have your first prison meal. And you're hungry. It's got to be even better than the jail food. It has got to be better.

Someone is going to touch you before you ever get down the hallway. Someone rubs your behind. Someone says, what's your name, cutie? Where you from? There are twenty-five inmates, at least, questioning you with perpetual questions like, "What are you doing time for? How much time did you get? Do you need some? I can give you something. Would you like this?" Others yelled, "I can help you with that. Come over here. Don't trust him. Come home with me."

When you get to mainline, when you get upstairs, you look, there are twenty guards walking around. None of them with a smile. The inmates behind the food bar are dressed in white. They're wearing hats and beard covers. It looks like the green beans cooked last week are still there. You wonder what in the world this is. Someone slaps you upside the head and says, "Shut up, there's no talking in the main room."

And you go to begin to eat. And you can't imagine how bad it tastes. All you hear is the roar of machinery, scraping of spoons and forks. And, sometimes, you hear a whisper. And you notice at certain tables, certain men sit at. And, sometimes, when someone sits at the table, someone has got their face slapped, because they sat in the wrong space. You understand there is a pecking order in prison. And you're the lowest pecker.

Night comes, but not quick enough. Now, you realize you're going to be counted, but you didn't know how often. You stand up to be counted at 4:00 PM. At 9:00 PM, you stand at your cell again. At midnight, they shine a flashlight in your eyes. At 3:00 AM, they holler at you, are you there? At 5:30, they wake you up and say it's time to go to breakfast. At 7:00, the cell doors slide open and time begins. At 9:00, you come back and you wonder will I make it through? What do I do now? When do I go to school? What do I earn? I've only been here one day. How long do I have? And it's only been one day. How many more do I have? That's your first day.

What Young Boys Face In Prison

I'm 17 years old. I'm new in prison. I have a long sentence to do. The first one in my cell is someone trying to give me something. I tell them I don't want it. The niceness went to something inside me that scared the hell out of you

The tattooed warrior said this to me, "Boy, you can't be here by yourself. You're going to need me to take care of you. You know, when I take care of you, you're going to take care of me. That's just how it is here. We take care of each other. You can't get out of here. There is 3,000 of us in here, each trying to make it through this day and you can't do it alone. You have to make a choice, boy." And he left.

Less than three minutes later, another hardened man appears in front of me.

"I'm here for you," the man said. Listen, "If you don't align with someone, someone will hurt you. I'll have your back. It doesn't cost much."

" What do you mean?" I asked.

"Your folks can send me a little money and I'll take care of you. You don't have to be bending over like that. You keep your manly things. You can be a man in here. You don't have to do that. I'll take care of your back for you." The hardened man said this factually.

You really do not understand but you are beginning to feel the strangeness.

The hardened man says, "Time to go to the yard"
The yard is the classroom for gladiators.

For the first time in your life you now understand that you're not ready for prime time and you're sick to your stomach.

You look out and there in one corner, there is a weight pile, where the strongest men of this prison gather. They are the biggest men you have ever seen. Any of them could break you in half, in a heartbeat.

You start to walk towards that area and someone says, "Where are you going boy? You ain't earned the right there. That's not yours."

So you stop.

You go to the other side, they're playing racquetball against the wall. You start to walk there. Someone says, "Where you going, boy? You don't belong there."

An officer walks up to you and says, "You're new here, aren't you son?"

The officer looks at you and states this like it was a simple fact of life. "You'll have to pick one."

You sit against the wall and wonder, what does he mean by, "You have to pick one?" Can't I live by myself? Can't I be my own man?

Within another heartbeat, there are three different people, asking "Where are you at?"

"What is your belief about this? What do you think is important? Do you want to make it through this?"

You look at them and there's more of them coming at you. You can't help but ask in the quiet of your mind, "Is there is a reason for the art gallery on their bodies?" Their whole story is tattooed on them. You wonder what it all means.

The glare of the eyes scares you. For the first time in your whole life, you understand the meaning of what fresh meat is. For the first time, you understand what valuing another human being really means. And what frightens you is, you understand. You have no value.

There was an old voice from behind you. He was a kindly gentleman, who looks old. He said, "Son, you need to get off your ass and out of here, you're not ready for this place. You don't have enough uhh to be here."

You ask him, "What do you mean by enough uhh?"

"Son, if you have to ask that question, get your ass off the yard and out of here. Go back to the education center. Go some place, because you don't belong here."

Every time you take a step, you look behind your shoulder. Every time you take a breath, you smell putrid. Every time you go to take a shower, you're never at ease because you wonder who is going to join you. Every time, you go to the bathroom, someone watches and you wait for the officer to flush. And you wonder, "Why?"

God, will this ever end?

A choice. Which group do I belong to? How do I survive? Where do I go? Who is telling me the truth and who is lying? How do I know which gang to belong to? Should I belong to a gang? My God. How do I learn? Who is here to teach me? Staff members? They can't help me. They know, it's not that they ignore it, they just can't stop it. After all, it's only one of them for every 250 inmates. How can they stop anything? They can do the best to keep this all inside. I have to find a way. I have to find a way.

I go to my counselor and I ask, "Can I call home?" He only laughs.

"I want to call home, I need to call my mom. You have a phone, please let me use it."

The counselor said, "You call collect and that is it son."

You yell, "Mom can't accept charges."

The counselor replies, "Then, you can't make a phone call."

"Can I call my attorney?" I ask.

"Does he accept collect calls?"

I'm isolated. Who do I... How do I survive?

Letters; Getting Mail

The first day I'm there, actually, I've been there a week. I know my mom has been waiting to write me every single day. And I know the officer is there. He's actually handing mail out. The highlight of my day. I know I've got mail. I used to get junk mail from school and junk mail from credit card companies. I hope I get junk mail today. I really would like to have a letter from mom, dad or my friends. I know my homies are going to write me or send me some money, I know they're concerned about me. I know they'll do it.

The officer hollers after the count at 4:00. He says its mail call. He stands up on a box and he reads a list of names and he's very articulate. He's made it alphabetical again. To speed the process up of Mail Call. He hollers out "Andrew." The next one down was "Edwards." And he hollered two more names out and there are five hundred men standing and only six letters passed out. Five hundred hopeful people. We'd all gather each day. I never seen more than six letters passed out at any one time. You don't understand. We are in the land of the forgotten. That's it.

The most powerful thing in life is seeing the emotional feeling of being forgotten played out in front of you each day. All of us show up for mail call because just once someone may call out my name.

What Can I Have in My Cell

I got my life organized now. Damn near a month, I've got things going my way. I could manage this time. I've got toothpaste, toothbrush. I've got clean underwear, clean shoes. I've got socks. I've got paper. I've got my whole life organized. In fact, I even got some things I shouldn't have, like some stolen cookies. And I've stolen some other items from someone else. I've pilfered things here and there. I made it pretty well through this maze of insanity. And suddenly someone says, get out of your cell. And there is an officer standing there. Shakedown time. He opens up my locker and he says, "Boy, come here. What is this?" What does it look like? It's cookies. And he takes them up and tells you to come over and put them in the toilet. Everybody else is laughing.

127

Whose cookies did I steal? He opens up some more and he says, "What are you, what is this? You can only have three bars of soap. You can't have four. And, besides this one, it's not what we issue here." He throws it in my commode and flushes it again. What little I had extra in life is taken again.

The officer goes through my underwear and socks. He unrolls everything and throws it on the floor. He takes my mattress and pulls it apart. He strips my bed. Everything that could hold contraband is taken apart. I have no letters. I have nothing except what I brought in with me for legal papers. He goes through each one and throws them on the floor.

"You can't do that officer," I said.

"Yes, I can," was his response. "You can't have anything that exceeds what you can put into a shoebox, boy. That's it," the officer said.

I now understand that I have "lost it all."

1

My Name is JosepH, I am a 24 yEAR old from ChicAqo, ILLinois. I AM currently on my 5th yEAR in the IowA Dept. of CorrectionS, I AM Writing because I would Like to Share a Little advice With those who at this Point in there Lives are heading to this Side of the fence. first Let me tell you a little about myself, I WAS born & raised in ChicAqo. Where I WAS attracted to the streets at a very young Age. By the time I WAS 14 yEARS old I WAS already a qang memeber and i had been arrested from everything as small as theft to Att. murdeR & firearm Possesion. I rememeber oldeR Guys who we looked up to in my Neighborhood would come home from Prison, I thought that WAS Cool and looked up to these Guys, who are Now mostley DeAd oR doing Life Sentence's. I found myself in and out of every Juvinile Inst. in the State of Illinois, I would get out and come right bAck, Prison always has a bed open, finally after this I turned 18 and would Listen to NO one, All I cared about

Z

was being down for my homeboys,
my gang, my hood. Little did I
know Destruction was close. I
begain to make frequent trips to
Florida where I found myself
at 18 with a Armed Robbery and
2nd degree Murder charges as
I sat facing Life in a state foreign
to me where I knew no one I
expected to be taken care of from
my homeboys back in Chicago,
well Im Still Waiting! also I
learned at o what I thought was
a down homeboy was going
to testify on my, this was my
main man, a real stand up cat
boy was I wrong, so I got
12 years mandatory, I was 18
when I came to the joint I
will be almost 31 when I am
released. So if your out there
wanting to be down, a gangster
whatever, you will either die or
be right here where me and about
2 million other people call home.
So I would like to tell you
a little bit about being in
prison   →

3

first of all I hope you own
earplugs because the Noise
Never quits (NEVER!!)
It will bring you to a breaking
point, (The intercom blaring)(Rapping)
cards and Dominos being slammed on
the table, screams & conversations
full of Lies. You also better
start to establish yourself a
Routine, because you will be told
when to Eat, sleep, and shit &
every other daily activity you might
do. But you can still try and be
a real dude with a fuck you
Attitude and thats when you
will start taking trips to solitary
confinement where you are alone
24 hours a day and you will be
handcuffed and strip searched
Just for your 3 A.M. Shower
once a week. In the Joint you
are No longer a son, a brother, a
student, a Carpeter or whatever
your a outcast of society a
fucking Number. You also better
be ready to fight, because you
will Align yourself to a click and
will be expected to handle your buisness
No questions Asked. Also I hope

131

2/

you don't mind Not being able
to touch, smell or have any contact
with a women, Aint None in here
homies, Just a bunch of men full
of hate, rage and sexual frustration
and believe me ~~there~~ prison is
Rampent with 0 homosexuals and
be ready to spend years with
these ~~people~~ who spread disease
and decelt in prison, I'm telling
you this is real Life Misery and
If you are Just thinking screw
this chump he don't know shit,
Well maybe we will Run into each
other one day in My world behind
Razor wire and bars, where there
is No love, I hope at least one
person will take heed to this letter
this shit Aint a game, Its real Life
your Life, and I truly hope you
Never see one of these places
or have to endure this misrable Life.
be there for your familys and
those who truly care for you and
don't be ~~fooled~~ into the same stuff,
I was mislead to believe because Its
Bull Shit!
Any   straight up · " PEACE "
Questions ?
→   JOSEPH
             Newton correctional Facility·
             Box 218
             New ton, Iowa 50208

132

CHAPTER NINE
Secrets for Parents

There is a powerful driving force inside every human being that, once unleashed, can make any vision, dream, or desire a reality."

—Anthony Robbins

10 Day Challenge

Dear Moms and Dads,

If you've taken the time to read this book, I truly want to commend you. You're one of the few that has begun to ask what can I do to help my son or daughter. To encourage you and support you, I would ask you to take the Ten Day Parent Challenge.

The Ten Day Parent Challenge outcome is to help you understand what is really going on with your teen, what patterns are they developing, who has real influence upon your teen, and what is really going on in your teen's life?

You will keep track of:

1. How much time do you talk with your teen in conversation each day? How many minutes do we converse each day?

_____

_____

_____

2. When does your conversation occur? Morning, evening, over the phone?

_____

_____

3. How much did we really talk? Be honest with yourself. This time, be brutally honest. Did you just say hi and goodbye?

_____

_____

_____

4. What kind of questions did you ask (Open or closed ended)? Were they simply yes or no questions? Do you need to clean your room? Have you cleaned your room? Yes or no? Did you make it to school? Yes or no? Ask some open-ended questions, so you might leave room for conversation, or, at least, the possibility.

_____

_____

_____

5. Find a moment to build your child's self-esteem. Find a moment to tell them you are proud of them.

_____

_____

_____

6. Identify your teen's greatest strength and describe it to your teen and how where it shows up.

_____

_____

_____

7. Think back remember a time when you had a special moment that you felt loved by either a parent, grandparent, aunt, or mentor — just that special time. Share that with your teen. Ask, "What was the moment you felt most loved in life?"

_____

_____

_____

8. Schedule a time to tell your child they make you feel special.

Appointment time: _____

9. The magic moments of life is the key. Schedule at least 2 times to simply play with your teen. Find a time to play, at least one day during the week — schedule a time to play with your teen. Whether it's going to watch them at a sports activity, but, play together. It will be the most treasured moments of your life. If there is an activity such as team coaching, boy scouting or girl scouting or something with your church organization, do something with them together .

Appointment times: _____

10 Schedule at least one meal a day with your Teen. Eating meals together is one of the building blocks parents can use to create a place that is safe to exchange ideas and the events of the day. Have dinner with them for 10 consecutive days. Having a meal with another human being is the second most intimate thing you can do in life. It will be the place where you can unveil their potential, where you can ask all the questions. It can be the place where you care and share the most. For ten consecutive days, have at least one meal a day with your child, where you both, by the way, you both have to sit down. Mom, Dad. You both have to sit down. You have it as a family unit.

"The more you try to control a teen, the less you can influence that teen." Control eventually leads to resistance, and resistance to rebellion. Make them feel important, because it's your time.

"Over Ears" Strategy

One of the most powerful secrets I've been given in life, as a parent, was the discovery of the power of "over ears." During this week, select a time where you and your significant other can whisper about how you really feel about your child's accomplishments. For instance, if they're getting a B in math, whisper how proud you are about them. Because, when a child hears a whisper, what do you think they do? They listen intently with their unconscious mind. When they understand that you're truly proud of them, not just verbalizing the words, it multiplies, it's power tenfold. It takes on a whole new level of meaning. I call it the "over ears" secret.

What do they really want?

In the quiet times of your home, list what behaviors your teen is doing that is driving you insane. Write them down on a separate piece of paper that cannot be seen. Look at the list, with this thought in mind: All behavior is either a cry for help or a loving response. Review the list. If it's something that's driving you insane, what is the teen doing? If it's a cry, they want you to pay attention to them. What's the real need these kids are wanting met? I've heard it tens of thousands of times, "If my mom and dad had only paid attention." They only want a moment, not a lifetime. You only have them for a short period. Do your best.

I would like to close with a story . . .

The holes in my fence

The old man loved his grandson. However, he knew that the young man's anger would some day be a problem. One day after a really bad display of petty anger he went to him and took him by the hand and asked him to come with him. Together they walked into the back yard towards a wooden fence. The old man instructed the boy to drive one nail into the fence for each time he was angry that day. At the end of the day there were 37 nails in the fence.

Gradually, the boy realized it was easier to hold his anger than it was to go out and drive nails into the fence. Finally, the day came when the boy did not lose his temper at all. He was proud and told his grandfather about it. His grandfather told him how proud he was of him and asked if he thought he was ready for part two on the lesson. Of course, after managing his anger so well he was ready for anything.

Together they walked to the fence and the grandfather handed him a hammer and asked him to now pull out the nails. There were hundreds of nails in the fence. He told him you don't have to pull them all today. Each day you are not angry come out and pull a few nails out. Weeks passed and finally he was able to tell his grandfather that all the nails were out of the fence. The old man placed his hand on his grandson's shoulder and told him how proud he was of him. He asked, "Are you ready to learn some more?"
"Of course," the teen replied.

"Look at all the holes in the fence, son. The fence will never be the same. You see, son, when we say things and do things that cause others pain in anger, they leave a scar just like the holes in the fence. It is as though we put a knife in an innocent man/woman and draw it out. It will not matter how many times we say we're sorry, the wound is still there. See the holes in the fence? See the light passing through? Those represent the holes you left in someone's hearts when you were angry. The strange thing, son, is that hearts will heal with each wound but as the wounds build deeper scars it prevents the love they have for you to fully be expressed."

About the Author

Don Clair

Don Clair has recently completed a 29 year career with the United States Government and the Department of Justice. Don did his undergraduate and graduate work at Drury College in Springfield, Missouri. He and his wife Roberta Jane have six adult children and are currently living in Waterloo, Illinois. During his tenure, his specialties included Counselor, Case Manager, Drug Treatment Specialist and Crisis/Intervention Negotiator. Over the past two decades, Don has also designed and delivered cognitive behavior coaching programs for individuals and corporations of all sizes. He has a long career of successfully working with the most difficult clients and accessing methods for establishing positive relationships and helping them achieve their visions. Specifically, Don created a model program that was called Seiter Residential Model (SRM) and has been referenced in the Correctional Management Quarterly. The SRM program focuses on accessing emotional leverage that produces lasting change with the inmate's behavior. Don's programs and trainings provide specific relationship skills for creating an atmosphere that allows rapport and influence to occur. In addition, for the past 10 years, Don has also worked with Robbins Research International as a Trainer at Anthony Robbins seminars. Don was asked to be a part of the International Council for the Human Rights of Children in 2005, held at Oxford University, in the United Kingdom.

Notes